I had been drinking with K[...]
afternoon when he told m[...]
North Korea. From what he [...] said it, I got the impression that Kevin knew deep down that it was all too good to be true; and as he droned on, at considerable length and with growing intensity, I was inclined to agree with him: it was, indeed, all too good to be true.

But it was during this conversation with Kevin, in a pub by the Thames on that hot summer day in 2009, that the whole extraordinary adventure began to take shape; in the space of a few short summer months there would be the promise of mountains of gold in North Korea; the takeover of Notts County Football Club (the oldest football league club in the World) and the bewildering circus world of Formula One Racing (we bought the BMW Sauber Formula One Team); I was to meet an astonishingly colourful cast of characters including Sven Goran Eriksson, Roberto Mancini, Peter Sauber, Bernie Ecclestone and Lord Mawhinney, Chairman of the Football League. We would make the front pages of the *Sun* and the

Guardian, the inside pages of newspapers all across Europe and we would cross swords with Regulators at the League and the City Takeover Panel; but given it was, indeed, all too good to be true after all, it would eventually end up in a wasteful blizzard of recrimination. It had all though started back there on that summer's day in 2009, in a pub by the river Thames with Kevin.

Kevin was a bluff, squat Mancunian who had made the first of his millions (soon to be billions) in the funeral business. Neither of us stood on ceremony. He had often told me the story of his historic running dispute with the owners of the poster site next to the Headquarter Building of his funeral homes in Manchester; one week the poster next door was for British Airways: *"We get you down under quicker"*; Leech's Funeral Homes Then, two weeks later, there was a poster for De Beers Diamonds: *"Watch your friends go green"* Leech's Funeral Homes. He thought it was funny. I did too. Anyway, he duly made his millions before selling up and retiring to Jersey. But he soon got bored with island life and went back into the markets with a drug patent which proved to be so wildly successful that it made him a Billionaire; he was the seventh Richest man in Britain; and from there he bought into the nascent dot com boom in the late 1990's before making millions more. But it was all on paper.

When the dot com bubble burst in 2000, as it inevitably had to, Kevin's bankers took the perverse view that all this paper was no longer good enough to act as security for the hundreds of millions they had lent him along the way; at that time they had lent him the money the paper had looked for all the world like burnished dot com gold. But it didn't look like gold after the crash; it just looked like paper. And that was where I came in. I was the lawyer that Kevin had turned to when his banks started to demand repayment of their money; some £300 Million in all. Kevin was struggling to find all this in ready cash.

For a while we managed to hold the banks at bay through recourse to a series of increasingly technical technicalities; but it didn't last long. It couldn't last.

Kevin went bankrupt in the end and when he did it was the biggest bankruptcy in Jersey history and it hit him hard. He went from King of the Island to social pariah overnight and I was with him every tortured step of the way. I saw people move away from him in bars and whisper together when he came into a room. The process made us friends in an entirely predictable way. We were like two old soldiers coming up together from out of the trenches, bloodied and scorched with smoke; bonded by the experience. As I have said, he was a good friend.

I remember in particular the day that the house of cards finally fell in on Kevin just before he was adjudicated bankrupt. A call came through on my mobile while we were sitting in a pub in Jersey looking out over Walter Raleigh's Castle, far out in the bay. Both of us had a pint of Guinness and we had just come from a wearing meeting with his Trustees. The sun was shining out on the white capped waves and there was a palpable sense of calm after the frictions of the day. But the call was from Citibank's Lawyers; they would be issuing a statutory demand as a precursor to the inevitable bankruptcy process unless Kevin paid them £20 Million that same afternoon. It was already 2 o'clock so we only had two and a half hours at most to get the funds together before the banks closed. Even if Kevin had £20 Million, which he didn't (he only had me), it was bound to be a close run thing.

As we finished our pints Kevin came up with an idea:

"I know where we can get £20 Million from."

"Do you now."

"Yes. I do. We can borrow it from James. He's less than half an hour away."

Like a couple of students looking to borrow beer money, we finished what was left of our pints and headed off in Kevin's car to tap James for £20 Million.

James lived in a House that looked as though it had been dismantled brick by brick from the set of *Dynasty* and re-built on the outcrops looking over the Jersey coastline; that second bit was actually true. What seemed most implausible in the whole edifice was the construction of the exterior gates; they took the form of a huge pot of roses that folded into itself on entry; the stems of the roses forming the railings once they were fully deployed and the pot disappearing into a narrow trench in the road to let vehicles through. I watched in fascination as the structure separated and folded into the ground. Kevin seemed to know its intricate movements by heart and made no comment at the obvious oddity of the process; or maybe his mind was elsewhere. It probably was.

We were shown into James's study by his butler and Kevin looked around its wood panelled walls with a weary, and to a certain extent worldly, sense of damp eyed disbelief:

"You wouldn't believe the stuff that's gone on in here."

I didn't ask him to explain what he meant.

Kevin had never lost his heavy Mancunian accent; he had a cleft palate from birth and so almost every word he spoke was lisped out with a visible effort of will. It wasn't what would be conventionally expected of a Billionaire; but there again, nothing about Kevin was. He looked like nothing so much as a malign dwarf or perhaps the star turn in Rigoletto; no taller than five foot five, virtually round and always dressed in a funereal black suit. His hair was thinning and running to rats tails and was oiled flat to the dome of his head; on a warm day, a day like today, you could smell the oil coming off him if you got too close. I could smell the oil on him now.

James kept us waiting. If this was a serious meeting, a meeting designed to raise a £20 Million credit line (a lifeline) in the next, what was it now, fourteen minutes, then on balance it would have been better if

7

we had not each had a pint of Guinness on an empty stomach within the last ten minutes. I was not feeling on top of my form and neither, I suspect, was Kevin. He was whispering in an undertone now, as though we were in church:

"It would make your eyes water if I told you what had gone on in here. You wouldn't believe it."

Again I declined to take the bait; I didn't want to know.

"You think he's *really* going to give you £20 Million?"

"We're mates. I've helped him out in the past. I think he will. The big thing is, and you need to back me up on this; when I tell him that £20 Million is enough to keep the banks quiet for a bit, tell him that's true, that it will keep them quiet. I want vintage Paul on this."

I didn't answer, not in words anyway. I frankly doubted whether even £20 million would keep them quiet; I doubted whether any of this was going to work anyway. It just felt a bit too wacky to be serious but there again a lot of what I had been doing with Kevin over the past year had been wacky; a lot of it had that faint, weird penumbra of other worldliness. Maybe it would work? For the want of anything more substantive to say, Kevin fell back into his refrain, still whispering hoarsely:

"You wouldn't *believe*........"

But this time he didn't have time to finish. The doors slid open and James came in; stooping slightly with age.

They greeted one another with the affection of the friends they obviously were; James took a seat opposite the two of us, behind his enormous and impressive desk; and unlike Kevin he didn't spend any time beating about the bush:

"What can I do for you Kevin?"

"Well, the big thing is James……….. *The big thing is*, I won't beat about the bush, I need £20 Million James."

By way of emphasis, and just in case James was likely to miss the point (which he very obviously wasn't) Kevin slapped the desk with the palm of his hand when he said *"£20 Million"*.

The request didn't seem to take James by surprise; but he was obviously having none of it.

"I can't do that for you, sorry Kevin."

Kevin's eyes instantly seemed to well up with tears as he looked around the room. He was avoiding eye contact with both of us now, seeming instead to be fixed on his own future. It didn't look as though I was going to be called on to tell James that everything was going to be alright after all. It was, indeed, becoming clear that everything was going to be very far from alright. This was going to be a threshold moment for Kevin and me.

In any event James was already ahead of us:

> "I don't think the bank is going to pull away on this Kevin, I spoke with them yesterday on the collateral position; it's going to take a lot more than £20 Million to get this to go away."

I thought that Kevin was going to start crying but he held himself together as best he could. Then with a heavy lisp he wrote his epitaph; there was a deep sigh that seemed to shake him to his core:

> "I suppose I'm fucked then."

He was indeed fucked. And then James told us, disarmingly, that he had already started shorting stock in Kevin's main operating companies on the assumption that he would shortly go bankrupt anyway. That's what friends are for.

We left without the £20 million he needed and the heavy leather wings of bankruptcy were finally to engulf poor old Kevin two weeks later.

As I have said, the whole process drew us together. We became close friends and I liked him a lot. To a certain extent we shared a common heritage.

I subsequently took Kevin through the ridiculously difficult process of securing his early discharge from bankruptcy in Jersey, and when he emerged from that two years later he set about finding another Project, one last venture into the Markets, one last dot com surrogate that would prove to the World that he still had it in him. That was all Kevin wanted; just to prove that he still had it in him, and then he would retire. In pursuit of this dream he had already tried investing in internet poker and he had also tried investing in an actual bricks and mortar poker club; and he had also tried investing in internet tax free shopping but none of those had set the world on fire (certainly not the poker club where I was regularly called over, at least once a month, to stop the second biggest shareholder from having a fist fight with the manager). So Kevin was now looking for something else that might ignite the world instead and that "*something else*" is what we were talking about outside the pub on this particular Friday afternoon in the summer of 2009. It was a very warm day and Kevin was obviously feeling the heat in his conventional black suit; every inch the retired undertaker; I could smell the oil on his hair and I remember squinting into the sun as Kevin set out cautiously for me the bare bones of his new project.

Through one of his offshore trust vehicles called Condor, Kevin had an interest in a London Bank called, naturally enough, First London. First London had been negotiating for some mineral rights overseas and now it had a letter of intent signed with the resource owner; now it was looking to exploit those assets and bring in some cash; lots of cash. The assets themselves apparently comprised a vast shelf of silver reserves. Kevin told me he had already handed over some £720,000 by way of fees to have these reserves valued; but now he was worried that it might all be a scam, an advance fee fraud lawyers would call it. He obviously still wanted it all to be true; I could see that; he wanted one last big deal before he retired and this was going to have to be it. For one thing he didn't have another £720,000 to hand over. But I still thought it had all the marks of an advance fee fraud and I told him as much. I also pointed out that if he was buying into silver reserves he ought to give some thought to what it would cost to get the stuff out of the ground; and then what it would cost again to ship it off to where it could be smelted and sold. I told him that in my view those were all points of difficulty (putting it mildly). Where was this silver anyway?

"North Korea."

"You mean *South* Korea?"

"No. *North* Korea. We've got a deal with the North Korean Government."

Kevin paused here but not for the same reason that I did; unlike me, he wasn't lost for words. Indeed he had an acronym for some of them:

"DPRK. The Democratic Peoples' Republic of Korea. We've got a deal to buy all their stuff. That's why I had to pay for the Survey Report; so that we know what the silver's worth."

I was taken aback; gobsmacked.

"Have you actually seen this Survey Report Kevin? Now you've told me what all this is about, £720,000 doesn't actually sound *enough*; not enough to pay for a full Survey of the entire silver resources of the North Korean State. Are you sure this isn't a scam?"

Kevin was giving every impression that he thought it was a scam. He looked to be sweating; it might be the heat of the Sun, to which he had his back; but he was canny enough to know when he had been taken in without my having to tell him; he was just too trusting to see it coming in the first place and now it was too late for him to back out. That was my take anyway. I told him he should ask for a copy of the survey report before he put any more of his money into the project. He said he would but I knew in my heart that he wasn't going to. As I say, he was already in too deep. Even when I asked him why on earth a London Bank should get involved in mining operations in North Korea, he could still persuade himself, as he went on to do, that it was all perfectly plausible and there was really nothing unusual about it at all; men in pinstriped suits digging out lumps of silver from the earth. But he had invested too much to let it go now. Not only his money; he had also invested all that was left of his reputation as well.

Two weeks later Kevin was back in London and we were both back at the same pub. It wasn't warm that day and the crowd had dissipated; and this time Kevin didn't look so nervous. He took a Bahraini banknote out of his pocket and snapped it in front of my nose:

"Here's my new business partner".

Snap, *snap* went the note between the thumb and finger of each of his hands.

"He even prints his own money."

Kevin was referring to the Finance Minister of Bahrain; he told me his "*business partner*" was now backing the North Korean Minerals Project; he told me the investment was enough not only to make Kevin feel comfortable that his £720,000 was actually well spent and safe after all but that he was on the verge, with his chums at First London, of reaping riches beyond his wildest dreams. The biggest silver reserves in the unfree world were theirs to do with what they would. He seemed to be in a state of euphoria which at least made a nice change from the last time I had seen him. Kevin pointed out to me why it was obvious that the Ruling Family in Bahrain should want to get involved in the North Korean Project:

"They love silver over there. They can't get enough of it. You should see the shops on the way out of the airport; they're stuffed with necklaces, rings, bracelets, plates; all of them made of silver. The big thing is, they like it better than gold even".

It sounded to me like a good reason to open a stall selling silverware at the airport in Bahrain but maybe not so good a reason to start trying to dig the stuff out of the ground half way across the world in North Korea. But on balance it was good to see Kevin back in a positive frame of mind; I had seen him low enough for long enough in and around the Greek Tragedy of his Bankruptcy in Jersey so I wasn't about to do anything to undermine his happiness now. Who was I anyway to say that the powers that be in Bahrain were incapable of recognising "a *riches beyond your wildest dreams project"* when they saw one; and I was pretty sure they were capable of having some pretty wild dreams; Kevin certainly was. He had always been quick to tell me that lawyers were the very last people to distinguish the real worth of a deal from the red tape and small print that it came wrapped up in. Maybe he was right.

Now the pace of things stepped up a gear or two and things were to get even odder.

Less than a week later, Kevin sidled into my Office off London's Cannon Street and asked me if he could spend some time working in our conference room. That was fine by me. He often used the room when he was in London. I was more amused than anything to be told later by Kevin, again we were making our way to the pub, that he had needed the room to make a top secret telephone call involving the former head of the Joint Intelligence Committee, Air Chief Marshal Sir John Walker, and a high level CIA contact:

"I obviously couldn't do it on the mobile in the street. These guys are serious. I needed to be security vetted before they would even speak with me. The big thing is, they don't mess around these guys."

Kevin clearly didn't think that *I* needed security clearance. Over a drink he told me that he had been mediating arrangements for a visit by Barak Obama to South Korea during the course of which the President was to make a closely scripted statement designed to open up diplomatic relations between the rest of the World and North Korea. Kevin told me archly that the Ruling Family in Bahrain had been behind the call and it was all designed to pave the way for First London's Minerals Project coming to the market. Getting North Korea into the fold of Western Nations was a necessary first step to allowing trade to take place in their Silver Resources. Kevin told me that he had been shown a report prepared by Goldman Sachs which stated that the unexploited reserves of silver in North Korea were among the largest in the World.

Barring the fact that it was comprised of silver, it seemed Kevin was literally sitting on a gold mine.

That bit about Goldman Sachs that Kevin had told me about proved actually to be true. Their report had indeed identified huge unexploited reserves of precious metals which were waiting to be mined and sold to the waiting world just as soon as North Korea's Pariah Nation status was removed. What Kevin had told me about Barak Obama's visit and what it was planned that he would say, actually made sense in that context. It was as sane as a white rabbit with a fob watch, but it still made sense.

And sure enough, Barak Obama did visit South Korea a month or so later; and whilst he was there he duly made a statement confirming the commitment of the United States to "*accent negotiations and inducements*" so as to convince North Korea of its need to return to the STP. He went on to highlight some of the "*inducements*" that Pyongyang would be offered in exchange for progress on the Peninsula's "*denuclearisation*"; Obama announced that he would be sending a special envoy to North Korea in December 2009 with a view to engaging in discussions aimed at paving the way for a resumption of STP in early 2010. U.S. Ambassador Stephen Bosworth subsequently also visited Pyongyang, on 8 December 2009, to begin bilateral negotiations; and in response to Obama's statement China then issued a statement of its own welcoming *"...the start of high level contacts between the United States and the DPRK...."*

And I had heard all about these overtures and diplomatic dance moves some two months earlier while walking with Kevin to All Bar One in Cannon Street. When the news broke, I seriously doubted that it could all just be a coincidence. Surely Kevin couldn't have *guessed* at what Barak Obama would be planning to say.

Oddly enough, my Firm would later act for Sir John Walker in connection with events during his time as a director of Notts County Football Club (of which more in a moment); Sir John had been introduced to us through Kevin, so it was actually quite possible that what seemed to be a preposterous lie on Kevin's part in late August 2009 may well have had the bones of truth in it; and maybe a bit more than bones. Sir John Walker had after all been the Head of the Joint Intelligence Committee at the time of Tony Blair's ill-fated *dodgy dossier*; he had also given evidence to the Hutton Inquiry on intelligence related issues. Sir John Walker was, and still is, a serious player in the Intelligence Sector. But at the time I took it as something of a harmless diversion that may or may not prove to be for Kevin's long term good; he might be spinning me a line but at least it was making him happy. Every time I saw him over this period he would pull the Bahraini banknote from out of his pocket, snap it open twice and tell me *"his mate"* was working to make them all rich. When I eventually saw the Press Reports on Obama's North Korean overtures, I started to think that Kevin might be right.

Except that the man on the Bahraini Banknote was not really Kevin's mate at all. There was an intermediary between them and he went by the name of Russell King.

Russell King used to live in Jersey and his children went to school with Kevin's little daughter so Kevin and Russell King had known each other pretty well.

Kevin told me that Russell King had left Jersey to work in Bahrain and that whilst he was there he had become very friendly with the Finance Minister; the man with control over Bahrain's almost limitless reserves of oil cash and the man, as it happened, whose face was on the Bahraini Banknote that Kevin kept showing me. It was Russell King who had orchestrated Bahraini involvement in the First London Minerals Project. As I was to find out later, but didn't know then, King had been imprisoned in Jersey some years earlier for his part in an Insurance Fraud involving an Aston Martin hidden in his garage; he had also orchestrated a Regulatory Fraud through a Jersey Company called Belgravia (in which Kevin was also involved) which led to the Jersey Financial Services Commission intervening in the Bank and Belgravia's resident director (Duncan Hickman) hanging himself in his garage; when news of that broke, but not before his assets were frozen by the Jersey Courts, Russell King had fled the Island to escape being arrested again. He had gone to Bahrain where, like a latter day Savonarola, he found himself at the very heart of the Bahraini Treasury; a fox in a hencoop. And now Russell King was going on a spending spree. First he had bought the entire Silver Reserves of North Korea and now Kevin was asking me:

"Is *Nottingham* very far from your home town?"

Kevin knew I was from Corby in Northamptonshire; both Counties began with an "*N*" and so naturally Kevin thought they were one and the same. I disillusioned him. In any event I pointed out that I had lived in London since 1979 so the proximity of Northampton to Nottingham was pretty much academic for me:

"But your *mam* and dad can get up to Nottingham in, what, an hour or so if they had to?"

"I suppose so. Why?"

"The *big thing* is, I can get you seats in a box for the Notts County games. Russell King's behind the Group that bought the Club."

Events were obviously moving very fast. Kevin told me that the investment in the Football Club was a *"small show"* of Bahrain's good faith; they had hoped that it would ease the way to the announcement of its much larger investment in North Korea's silver reserves. There was otherwise a worry that the good name of the Gulf State would be potentially tainted by its massive investment in what was still a Pariah State. I could see that. At least in the first few weeks, buying an English Football Club can make you popular and it can certainly generate headlines. Kevin was keen to ensure the integrity of his investment. So too, it seemed, was Russell King and those in the Gulf State who were behind him. The investment in Notts County was a good way of doing that.

The news of the Notts County takeover came hard on the heels of the call Kevin told me he had with the CIA and MI5 and the public statements that corroborated what he told me he had discussed with them; and that was on top of the disclosure of Kevin's connection with the Bahraini Investment Office (now substantiated through his connections with Russell King); then there was the billion dollar contract with North Korea; and coming on top of all that, it was the Bahraini interests represented by Russell King that had bought an English Football Club (only a little one admittedly but, as Kevin kept telling me, it was the oldest football league club in the World); that sounded as though maybe it wasn't all pie in the sky after all. Maybe a London Bank *was* about to go into the North Korean Mining Sector although, in fairness, what Kevin told me next punctured the balloon of credibility a little:

"They've signed up Sven Goran Eriksson to take over as Director of Football at Notts County. You just watch, within four seasons Notts County will be in the Premiership".

Kevin suggested that I put a bet on with William Hill.

That little piece of pie in the sky rapidly put my feet back on the ground; the former England Manager and bon viveur taking over at Notts County? Eriksson was a genuinely serious player on the world stage, having had a glittering career at both club and international levels. Pull the other one.

Kevin was obviously losing his grip.

Except, of course, that he wasn't losing his grip at all; he was deadly serious and, which was much more important, he was also right. Sven Goran Eriksson was indeed on his way to Meadow Lane; home of Notts County Football Club.

I found out that he was right while I was lounging around in the reception area at my office trying to find something interesting to do; the announcement flashed up ticker style on the television screen. It was big news and Sky News was covering it as a scoop; their broadcast was being televised live from Meadow Lane. The rolling banner at the bottom of the screen told the story but there was also a talking head on screen that was saying the same thing over and over again; I could almost hear it lisping with Kevin's

Mancunian brogue. Amazingly, beyond all expectations and as the latest link in the strange chain of developments fed out to me by Kevin over the past month, the news was breaking that a Bahraini Consortium had bought Notts County and that it had appointed Sven Goran Erickson to be its Director of Football. There he was, the man himself, Sven Goran Erickson, being interviewed on how excited he was to be embarking on the *"Project"* with the backing of the seemingly limitless resources of a Gulf State at his disposal.

Kevin had been right. It was almost shocking.

My relationship with Kevin was too close and he was too excited, not to say smug, at the media storm breaking around his camp for me to be kept out of the limelight for long. So I wasn't particularly surprised when I received a text message from him a few days later:

"I've landed you the big one."

That was how he put it: "*the big one*". I had already arrived at a state of mind where it seemed presumptuous any longer to set boundaries to Kevin's ambitions. What he meant was that my firm, my little Law Firm, would be instructed as lawyers to act in commoditising the agreements under which the North Korean Silver Reserves were to be exploited by what I still understood at that time to be the Bahraini interests Russell King was fronting. It is difficult to overstate the scale of this projected transaction when set against the paucity of my firm's resources. We had four corporate lawyers on our staff; all of them perfectly good lawyers and all of them with a track record of handling day in day out private company stuff with perfect competence; but not something on this scale.

I say that as though they had a lot of work to do otherwise. They didn't. For the vast majority of the two years they had been with my firm they had done virtually nothing at all; week after week, month after month they spent almost all of their time in writing updates for the website and taking their chums out for lunch in a fruitless effort to generate work. The litigation work of the firm had floated its business and it was litigation that had kept it afloat ever since. The corporate lawyers had grown fat and idle on that success. Well, here was a chance for them to pull their weight. At least that is what I thought. We had, after all, landed the big one.

But "*the big one*" proved to be a lot bigger than even Kevin had led me to expect. When I met the following day with his business partner, Derek Tread, I was given a term sheet for the proposed transaction which involved a special purpose vehicle called Swiss Commodity Holding AG (we always knew it as "SCH"; at least we did before it changed its name three times to avoid its creditors and then re-domiciled to the Marshal Islands so as finally to avoid the rest of the world as well); SCH would be buying the entirety of North Korea's mineral reserves; all of it, lock stock and barrel, from its coal to its copper; from iron ore to zinc and, yes, even its entire reserves of uranium.

I knew that if the Bahraini interests were indeed buying up the entire uranium reserves of North Korea (not to mention all of its other mineral resources as well) then this would make for a much bigger story even than the takeover of Notts County Football Club. It would be a bigger story than Sven Goran Eriksson; and that was saying something.

The plan as it was explained to me by Derek Tread at the briefing meeting was for Russell King's Bahraini interests, held through SCH, to purchase the entire issued shareholding in First London so as to combine the supposed might of the Bank's financial resources with the depth of North Korea's Mineral wealth. That would be a formal prelude to the enormous transaction comprised of SCH's own listing on the London Stock Exchange. I was told that instead of SCH paying actual cash for the First London shares (which were issued on the London AIM market), the asset value of SCH's contract with North Korea would be used as a massive barter payment to buy out the existing shareholders in First London. This process, using shares rather than cash by way of payment, would require the approval of the City Takeover Panel in London before the transaction could be completed.

It was what London calls *"blue book work"* which is for the most part complicated and arcane; very much the territory of corporate specialists.

It was so complicated, indeed, that it quite simply terrified all four of our corporate lawyers. Having had nothing to do for over a year; literally nothing to do, these lawyers were now being asked to orchestrate a multimillion pound takeover structured in compliance with Blue Book rules and subject to prior approval from the Takeover Panel. The more senior of them were not slow in telling me that the firm was simply not geared up for this type of work; and she was right. That did not especially fill me with confidence as the intention, according to Derek Tread, was that we should move on from the takeover to deal with the SCH Listing; which was a multi-billion pound transaction: in terms of market capitalisation, it was a bigger transaction than Exxon's agreed takeover of

Mobil Oil in 1999. It was bigger than the RBS Takeover of ABN Amro Bank in 2007 (a transaction which was so big that it sent RBS into a spiral collapse which helped to destabilise most of the World's financial markets). The SCH follow on listing was simply massive, there was no other word for it; and if my corporate colleagues thought the initial First London takeover was terrifying, how would they handle *that*?

The cyclopean scale of the proposed SCH Listing would make the Moon landings look like a trip to Nandos.

But first, as I say,, we were required to deal with the starter transaction which would be the acquisition of the entirety of First London's shares by way of a reverse takeover; SCH would pay £163 million for the shares and we would act on behalf of SCH for the purpose of putting the documentation, primarily the public offer document, together. I freely admit that I breathed something of a sigh of relief on learning that we would be acting for SCH rather than First London on this initial transaction; I had already had enough of Derek Tread snarling at me, indeed he was to carry on snarling over the next few days; sometimes barking too because he was not, as it happens, a particular fan of the legal process.

After I had finished my meeting with Derek Tread I sent one of our corporate lawyers over to First London's Office to scope out an expanded term sheet and set out some parameters for the no doubt extensive due diligence that would be necessary. She came back from that meeting in a state of denial and hard on her heels I received an angry call from First London saying that she lacked the necessary *"spirit of adventure"*; they had found her unwilling to roll her sleeve up and crack on with the Project, instead she was said to have betrayed an unfortunate tendency to get bogged down in jargon and red tape. That was what they said; jargon and red tape. She was apparently simply bogged down in the stuff.

The complaint was being made by First London's in house lawyer; which I thought was particularly odd because essentially he was criticising her for behaving too much like a lawyer. But she *was* a lawyer; and his criticism that she was placing too much emphasis on formality (seemingly with an utter disregard for making everyone as rich as possible as quickly as possible) ignored the fact, at least as I saw it, that formality is the bread and butter fare of lawyers as well; I would be surprised if she *hadn't* been interested in the formalities. That was her job.

But this was a refrain which I was to hear over and over again from First London over the subsequent weeks and months; and as time went on I came to realise that what was required in routine dealings with First London was not so much a spirit of adventure as a padded cell.

In the short term, however, I managed to stiffen the required backbones by effectively contracting out the fear. I arranged for the complex Blue Book Work to be carried out under our aegis by the London Office of an American Law Firm, Milbank Tweed. We chose them because the corporate lawyer in question was married to one of Milbank Tweed's London partners. Milbanks certainly had enough bodies on the ground to get the work done and as this was less than a year after the catastrophic collapse of Lehman Brothers, very few of those bodies had anything else to do in the way of mergers and acquisitions work anyway. The Milbank lawyers fell on the SCH Project with relish, like a dog on raw meat and for a very short time our tiny law firm was courted as though we were the keepers of the flame, which in a way we were. The Bahraini connections promised a pipeline of substantial work which was not dependant on debt funding at a time when debt funding (with its range of evil acronyms, CDS, ABS and MBS) was seemingly dead in the water. The advantage of oil backed wealth after all was that at least the money was real. Look where Barclays went for help in 2009 when the only other alternative was the British Government. They went to the Gulf.

Kevin Leech and, to a much larger extent, Derek Tread had both told me in very vigorous terms that they were unhappy with the quality of our home grown corporate lawyers. The constant complaint was that they (our lawyers not Leech and Tread) couldn't see the wood for the trees; that they had been talking about Circulars and Opinions, and approvals from the City Takeover Panel, which would surely get in the way of completing the transaction in the seven days that First London had allowed. I told both of them that there was no chance of a seven day completion in any event; Takeover Panel approval would undoubtedly be required and that would take months, not weeks. Having Milbank Tweed involved in the process would, I thought, give us the necessary heft and bulk to deal with those kind of complaints in the future; not to mention the fact, which was also undoubtedly very important to me at the time, that to a man and woman my corporate lawyers were telling me consistently that Milbank retainer was absolutely indispensable to the project. So that was the way we went.

A meeting was arranged with Russell King for the following day at the Dorchester Hotel in Park Lane so that he could approve all of this; and, in particular, approve our acting on behalf of SCH on the First London takeover. I had not met King before and as he was the guiding mind behind SCH it was obviously necessary to meet him early on. Derek Tread was not, after all, in any kind of client relationship with my firm, whatever the appearances might have been to the contrary. It was, though, all terribly exciting.

Kevin Leech had arrived at the Dorchester early the next day and he was already busy playing the part of master of ceremonies by the time I got there; he materialised seemingly from nowhere as I pushed through the revolving doors; his hair, as usual, slicked back and oiled up into several rats' tails Kevin said hello to me with theatrical, wide open arms:

"They're here. I've put a good word in for you. The big thing is, be on your best behaviour now, no fooling around."

"*No* fooling around? That's my long suit."

He glared at me with mock paternal warning:

"*No* fooling around.......they're all back there."

He had spun on his heels as he spoke and was pointing to the back of the long reception area that ran off from the lobby into the gloom of the hotel proper.

It was obvious from the crush of people in the far corner, the corner towards which Kevin had gestured, that this was not going to be a normal business meeting. For one thing the two prime movers who doubled as the honey pot for the milling crowd, Russell King and Nathan Willett, were sitting not at a desk or a table but were each lounging indolently on a huge, round ottoman construction which would be wholly in character as the centrepiece for the Sublime Porte in 1814; Russell King, in particular, looked as though he had been transported directly from Nineteenth Century Constantinople, his elephantine figure was leaking out all around him as he smiled at his suitors. That was when I got my first sighting of his trademark walking cane which he held rigid at the dead centre of his bulk, resting both hands on its polished amber knob; he undoubtedly needed the cane to prop up his huge bulk as he moved around, but as I got to know him I got to know also that King thought of the walking cane as an essential prop for his fictions. Like a white cat for a Bond Villain.

As I walked across the room towards them, sinking into the thick carpet as I did so, I recognised the Duke of Kent and Tim Yeo coming the other way towards me. They both looked as though they had already been promised what they had come for. Both were smiling in a way that only the City of London finds commonplace. Kevin, of course, was keen for me to know who they were; so once we had safely passed the two of them and they were out of earshot he put a claw on my shoulder and dragged me closer to him:

"Do you know who *they* are?"

"I do Kevin, yes."

It would he hard not to know. Tim Yeo had been a central player in the cash for questions debacle of the

1990's which had made all the front pages for all the wrong reasons for a month or so and his mate was the Grand Master of the English Freemasons, President of the Boy Scouts and sometime Earl of St Andrews. He is also the Queen's Cousin. Yes, I had seen them both around if only in the Papers; I knew who they were.

Given my immediate recollection of where and why I had first seen Tim Yeo (on the receiving end of cash for questions allegations), I did not draw a great deal of inspiration from *his* presence; but I do remember thinking that if Russell King and Nathan Willet were being courted by British Royalty (and the President of the Boy Scouts into the bargain) there was no reason to suspect that everything was anything other than above board. It certainly made it more credible that Russell King should himself be associated with a member of the Bahraini Royal Household.

As the Duke and the MP skated off and out of the doors behind me, I marched on with Kevin to be introduced to Russell King and Nathan Willett.

They were both charm personified.

Kevin introduced me as his *"European Lawyer"* and a man very much to be relied on in a crisis. His eagerness to please was as oily as what was left of his hair. But Russell King took it all in his stride anyway and smiled grandly at me from his ottoman. It occurred to me that he wasn't at a table because there wasn't a table big enough in London to accommodate his distended frame. Perching on a glorified footstool was probably as comfortable as things could get for him. He reached out his hand of sausages to me and I shook them as best I could. He had what my mother would call a wall eye; flat and staring the wrong way from the conversation; his peculiar look could well put others off, but I had spent the last six years working with Kevin Leech, so there wasn't much in the line of human deformity that was going to throw me off my stride now.

"Nice to meet you", I lied.

As an ice breaker I added that we were all excited by the takeover of Notts County Football Club; I mentioned how pleased I was (another lie) at his coup in getting Sven Goran Eriksson to sign up as Director of Football of the Club. Even in retrospect, however, that was quite an achievement. Notts County might be the oldest Football League Club in the World but at the time it was struggling to avoid relegation into the oblivion of the Conference; today it is struggling to avoid the oblivion of relegation back *into* the league that it was to come out of in that first year under Eriksson's stewardship. But, to be fair to him, Russell King was very keen *not* to take any of the credit. He assured me that he had nothing to do with the purchase of the Club and that he was not involved in its day to day operations. At the time I took this to be an excess of modesty but I was later to become familiar with the full rigours of the "*fit and proper test*" as applied by the Football League which made King's seeming modesty more understandable; not to say less praiseworthy with the full benefit of hindsight (more of that later).

Willett was not as memorable from this first meeting. Like Russell King, Willet was an obvious candidate for weightwatchers, but more in the rugby club sort of way. You could almost understand how he had got so bulky (too much lager and too many fish suppers) whereas King's dystopian approach to food was simply beyond human understanding. Willett also distinguished himself from King by adopting an easy bonhomie which was plainly designed to present him as one of the lads. Not like Russell King; King was far more monarchical in his own, peculiarly contrived persona. He bubbled at me through his thick lips:

"Pleased to meet you too Paul."

It was almost a surprise to hear King speak English. I had spent my childhood and early adult life accustomed to seeing and hearing Jabba the Hut being rendered into English only with subtitles.

"Very nice to meet you", I lied again.

I then fell seamlessly into a pitch for my firm to act on the transaction. I explained that we worked off a small but highly skilled platform; just as good as the major City Firms but without any of their bullshit (the standard small firm pitch meaning we had to work off a small platform because we didn't have a bigger one). I was surprised that each of King and Willet seemed to be taking it in without question; I was accustomed to encountering more of a struggle than this from prospective clients. I explained that if we needed to bring in more bodies on the job then we could; if the platform was too small, we could bring in assistance from another City Firm. That was the American Firm that I had already enlisted to help out as needed: Milbank Tweed. Russell King nodded; he was happy for us to do that if we needed to. Willett was nodding too. It seemed he was happy as well.

Both of them instantly and without question agreed to this modified retainer; indeed, King had rapidly moved on and was now scoping out the full enormity of the Project:

"There are five classes of resources", he explained: *"Anthracite and Carbon based minerals"* (Coal to you and me); *"Iron and Steel"* (obviously); *"Precious Metals"* (Gold and Silver; King explained this made it useful that they would be mining so close to the *"Silver hub of Singapore"*); *"and Commoditised metals"* (which, for reasons which are still beyond me, meant copper, tin and nickel and the like).

As he went through each of these resource classes King counted them out on his thick, stubby fingers (which went well with his thick stubby head). He folded each of his fingers back in turn as he did so, like a child learning to count; and, finally, he was left gingerly holding one thumb, like the pin of a grenade:

"And of course then there are the Fissile Resources, Uranium and Plutonium and the like but we won't be dealing with those in the Circular; not for the time being. There are some things you can't mention in the same breath as North Korea without the Press getting into a froth".

Russell King clearly wasn't a man given to understatement.

What he had just told me was that SCH had indeed bought the entire mineral resources of the North Korean State. They hadn't, of course, paid for them; that wasn't part of the deal. But Russell King confirmed that the notional purchase price in the agreement with North Korea was £80 Billion which was a long way from chickenfeed; it was all pretty much as Kevin Leech had told it to me. He hadn't been joking after all. As for Swiss Commodity Holding itself, King wanted to make clear that he had nothing to do with the operation of that company (just as he had told me so disarmingly that he had nothing to do with the operation of the Football Club); SCH was Nathan Willet's company; him and his dad were the two non-resident directors; they were, I was told, both big in Dubai Construction Projects. Willett duly nodded his agreement with what King had just said. SCH was *run* by Nathan Willett and his dad. But it was *owned* by various members of the Bahrain Royal

Family through an offshore company called Qadbak. These were the shadowy creatures for whom we would act on the transaction; we were to represent SCH in the First London takeover; which would be a precursor to SCH itself securing a listing on the London Stock Exchange (that of course was the enormous transaction that Kevin Leech longed to bring to fruition; unlocking as it would a tidal wave of cash referable to its £80 billion asset value.

That information, tediously delivered though it was by Russell King, actually mattered quite a lot for me because I knew I would need to carry out money laundering checks on my client which, I assumed correctly, was going to be SCH; I would need to know who its directors and shareholders were in addition to the Willett father and son double act:

"Who are the other directors of Swiss Commodity Holdings?"

"*Holding*. Singular".

As I was to learn later, this was a familiar Russell King ploy. By pointing out that the company was called *"Holding"* and not *"Holdings"* he hoped to make the person asking the question (on this occasion me) look ill-informed or even stupid depending on how abrasively he phrased it (he was actually reasonably polite with me that morning but the comment still made me instinctively pull away from my enquiry which, of course, was exactly what Russell King's intended).

I had in fact thought up until that very moment that the lack of an "s" at the end of the company's name was a typographical error on the incorporation forms; but the tone of interjection made me pause nonetheless:

"I need to know who the SCH shareholders are as well".

"We'll get that over to you this afternoon Paul".

"And I'll need someone to sign the retainer letter".

That was the formal contract that would regulate the relationship between City Law, my Firm, and Swiss Commodity Holding.

"No problem Paul. Send it over and we'll have that signed this afternoon too".

Fine, I thought. That all went easily enough. A bit too easily if anything but I never thought *that* at the time. It seemed better certainly for my firm to be acting for the SCH side of things than First London who were behaving like a bag of cats.

Willett told me that it had been a BVI company called Munto, which had purchased Notts County Football Club. He told me in the beaten path of conversation, he was leaning in much closer to me now and the others had started to talk about something else; he told me that he was a director of the Club and that along with Sven Goran Eriksson he was on the lookout for a replacement manager, someone more in keeping with the newly minted status of the Club. They were meeting with Roberto Mancini next. Willet pointed Mancini out and sure enough there he was waiting at a side table. Mancini smiled back when Willett caught his eye and threw him a brief wave of one hand; almost shyly, as though he either didn't want to be noticed or was wary that he was interrupting Nathan Willett's conversation with me.

My thoughts were in any event interrupted by Kevin Leech who was now louder and more ebullient than anyone else in our small group. He positively bubbled over with enthusiasm. What would the Papers say, he asked, when they found out that their company (SCH was always *"their company"* for Kevin) had bought the entire Uranium and Plutonium resources of North Korea. He wasn't alone. They were all four cackling away now like the witches in *Macbeth*. Riches were in the air; riches beyond their wildest dreams and they were conjuring them up between them. I didn't know how many noughts there would be on the purchase price and I was trying to work that out in my head: I know now, there are ten of them with an eight in the front. Leech lisped in his thick Mancunian accent:

"We can make our own fucking *atomic bomb*."

Russell King suddenly went serious when he heard this. He lent in close, shaping a pantomime conspiracy; it was almost too absurd:

"Not so loud Kevin, we can't let news of this get out. The North Koreans will go spare if it gets out that we've bought their uranium."

Kevin fell into line immediately. They all agreed, as though they were taking a solemn covenant. It was best to keep it all secret. From then on in what was left of the conversation, everything was conducted in a stage whisper. We ought to think of a code name suggested Willett; what about *"Silver"*? But that wasn't much of a code name given SCH would be buying mountains of actual silver; it was a bit off a giveaway, like calling the search for Lord Lucan "Project Lucan". We agreed, all of us, to give the question of a more appropriate code name some thought. If I could do it again now, with the twenty twenty benefit of hindsight, I would suggest *"Project Bullshit"*; but those were simpler times then. At the time I still believed that what they were telling me might be true.

Later on that same day someone in my office, for reasons which I cannot now remember, decided to use the codename *"Fluoride"* for the Project; and *Fluoride* it was.

So we had a codename: Project Fluoride; the takeover of First London by SCH for a stated consideration of £163 million. I didn't speak to the Takeover Panel myself at the time but I understand they expressed some surprise at the deal when they were first told about it; particularly when they were told how big it was going to be.

It looked like being an awfully big adventure for all of us.

Curious company

Although the initial takeover of First London was very sizeable in itself (never mind the projected market capitalisation of the follow on SCH listing), the level of due diligence which was being made available to us by First London was desultory. I was by this time, this was within a matter of days of the Dorchester meeting, getting used to being told by First London's people that they would not put up readily with nit picking lawyers; and a steady stream of our own nit pickers were duly returning day by day to my office after a "get pragmatic" mauling from Derek Tread. It was especially dispiriting because they were not even being mauled by their own client; they were being mauled by the other side, counterparty. The client at least was paying us for the privilege to maul demand. It was making each of them, man, women and boy alike, especially irritated and they were sparing no opportunity to tell me about it; and they were telling me a lot about Keith Brentford.

Keith Brentford was the in house lawyer (for want of a better term) at First London. As First London were pretty much at the centre of most of what was to happen over the course of the next few months, it may be worth saying something about them here.

It is strange to remember it this way but until 1979 *anyone* could set up and operate a bank in the United Kingdom without any regulatory oversight of any kind. There was no regulator; and neither was there any governing legislation to stipulate what you could or couldn't do with your bank, and neither were there any rules about what could or couldn't be done to persuade or beguile trusting members of the public to deposit their life savings with you. Anyone could set themselves up, advertise themselves as a bank and accept deposits from anyone stupid enough to hand their money over. Margaret Thatcher changed all of that and although the supervisory regime which she devised for the financial sector delivered in rapid order the financial catastrophes that were Johnson Mathey, Barlow Clowes and BCCI, it also closed down the opportunities which had undoubtedly existed up until then for the footloose and the rogues. So that had to be a good thing. The regulatory and compliance industry is now one of the biggest sectors of the economy. But even in its fully developed format this regulatory structure still has its fringe elements and at the time Notts County was looming into the sights of Russell King, that fringe was the working climate of the curious little institution that was First London.

Based in St James's Square in London (appropriately enough) First London was an absolute hot bed of half-baked schemes and lame assemblies; projects of the most fanciful kind thrown up by the dot com boom found a natural root there; Kevin Leech found a natural root there. Kevin had podgy fingers in half-baked pies ranging from first minute dot coms to on-line airline timetables. And, as I have said, he lost virtually all of it when the bubble burst in 2000. Save for his relatively insignificant trust funds, Kevin lost his billions when he became one of the highest profile bankrupts of the crash. He was very much a fixture at the St James' Square Headquarters. I remember telling him, after several months of fighting an intense and ever less successful rear-guard action trying to fend off his creditors, that although the game was very likely up (as it proved to be), his fall would not attract the kind of attention and opprobrium that in his deepest fears he felt it must; the world was worried about other things. His bankruptcy, I told him, was not high up on the world's list. I couldn't have been more wrong. The very next day he was front page news in the Times: "*A Billionaire Falls to Earth*" was the headline; and as if that wasn't bad enough there was a graphic of Kevin's portrait falling off a wall. Clearly the world did care after all. In the result I think he took to spending more and more of his time at St James' Square; to hide away from the world amongst the lunacy.

Once he had acquired a taste for sloshing around in tech stock, which he did a few years before the bubble burst, Kevin Leech had inevitably been drawn into the orbit of First London; and, as part of the same gravitational pull, to his old mate and First London's driving force, Derek Tread.

Derek Tread was a barrow boy to bubble kind of creature and his earthy simplicity was itself I suspect a natural match for Kevin's wayward charms. The two had teamed up in as part of a natural, money making simplicity and they teamed up again for their projects with Russell King. That was how I became involved with Derek Tread. King was the catalyst.

It would be difficult to imagine any team set more loosely in its rails.

I suspect that as part of all this, as the in-house lawyer who was supposed to hold it all together, Keith Brentford was required to fight in earnest with Derek Tread daily, hourly even, to bring some stability to the ship of fools. As the company's in house lawyer that was his job and I am sure that he did it as best he could. But it cannot have been easy. Tread had a violent temper and he was not slow to unleash it at the slightest suggestion that he might not be getting his way. He regularly reduced several of my staff to tears so Lord knows how Keith coped with the daily frictions he undoubtedly endured. And with the best will in the world, Keith Brentford was doing little if anything to control these wilder excesses. As most apparatchiks tend to do, he seemed to cope mostly by telling Derek Tread that the mountainous difficulties that lay in the way either didn't exist at all or that they had simply been made up by some unhelpful outsider (usually a lawyer was the villain, including us); made up to stop the deal getting done. Compliance with even the most basic legal requirements was routinely dismissed at First London as *"deal prevention"*; money laundering checks (fundamental to any legal process) were lightly tossed aside as *"form filling"* and whole tranches of the *City Takeover Code* were airily rejected as *"legalese"*.

But the Takeover Code was, of course, the immediate problem and there was no avoiding it.

As I have said, Russell King and First London had planned between them to structure the North Korean deal as an acquisition by Swiss Commodity Holding of the entire issued shareholding in First London

Bank. That was still the plan. But First London was listed on the London AIM market and its shares were traded by members of the public; so buying the shares required a public offer to be made by SCH (it would have to issue a public Offer Document to do that); and the terms of that offer, down to the last detail would have to be first approved by the Takeover Panel in London. So, whatever the Tread/Brentford Axis thought of legal compliance and legalese, however high their contempt might otherwise be for "deal preventing" external advisers, it would simply not be possible to ignore the blue book. The essential practical issue which they faced, of course, was that SCH did not have any money of its own to buy the First London shares; and I mean no money at all, it was not an operating company and so it could not afford to buy a second hand Ford Fiesta let alone produce £163 million in cash. It had been incorporated only a few months beforehand in Geneva and it didn't have two Swiss Francs to rub together. But of course what it did have was non-cash assets; it had, as I had been told at the Dorchester the previous day, the exclusive rights to the entire mineral reserves of North Korea; and that was big bucks in anybody's book.

So the plan was to run the transaction without paying any cash at all; the shareholders in First London would instead be asked to agree to sell their shares in exchange for some shares in SCH itself? Those shares would then give the First London existing constituency of shareholders a direct interest in the North Korean assets held by SCH which would be worth more than mere money; they would literally have an interest in a gold mine.......and a silver mine, and coal mines and tin mines and copper, lead, manganese and nickel and of course (but never to be mentioned), mines full or uranium too; all kinds of mines. Easily worth more than the £163 million that SCH was planning to offer for the First London shares.

That, at least, was the plan.

The Blue Book rules certainly allowed non cash assets of that kind to be offered in exchange for shares, but in that case the assets themselves have to be valued; and the Offer Document which is then issued to the public prior to the transaction being completed would have to include, in general terms, a certification from an independent expert (usually an accountant) setting out what the value of the assets is and how the valuation had been arrived at. For obvious reasons the Takeover Panel are pretty firm on compliance with that Rule. Members of the public might otherwise be beguiled into giving up their valuable shares in public companies in return for any old moonshine and pumped up tat. So that was the reason for the particular emphasis that was being put on the need for strict compliance with these Blue Book principles; especially the need for an asset valuation and Takeover Panel approval of the terms of the Offer document itself. It was simply not possible to ignore those requirements and the transaction was going nowhere for as long as they were constantly being dismissed (as they were by those at First London who we were dealing with) as "legalese" and "red tape".

The question of valuation, a *formal* valuation, of the assets in North Korea was of course the very question which I had asked Kevin Leech to think about when we had met outside the pub a couple of months earlier. So what had we found out since? How were we going to answer it in a way that would satisfy the Takeover Panel? What, in other words, were these North Korean assets *actually* worth?

Well, taking stock, we were not entirely without some working information on the issue even at that early point in the transaction.

First and foremost, we had been given a copy of the agreement which had been entered into between SCH and the North Korean Government and it did indeed allocate exclusive rights to exploit the free reserves of the nation for a period of twenty years; all of them, from aluminium to uranium (which we were, of course, never to talk about). There was nothing inauthentic about the Agreement; it had been formally signed on behalf of the North Korean Government; it had been registered, as it was appropriate that it should be, with the United Nations in Geneva as a Bilateral Trade Agreement; it had an authentic North Korean stamp and it was, as lawyers might say, "internally consistent". So that was all good.

But what were the assets actually worth?

On that front we had the Goldman Sachs report from 2005 and the answer, according to their report (it obviously carried some weight bearing in mind its genesis), was very many billions of dollars; that was in itself unsurprising but it was obviously, and more importantly, way, way more than the amount SCH was planning to pay for the First London Shares. So that was good too. Whilst it wouldn't do as a pounds shillings and pence, spot on valuation for use as certification in the Offer Document, if the assets were worth ten or twenty times more than the offer price for the shares (which it looked like they were), then the Blue Book opinion could say that, or something like that, and provided the Takeover Panel were happy, an imponderable to be fair, then the First

London shareholders could make up their own mind on whether to accept the offer or not.

And there was something else as well; something more colloquial by way of asset comfort.

We knew that Sven Goran Ericksson had an agreement with Notts County that he would receive shares in SCH in return for taking over as Director of Football at the Club. Ericksson was under the impression that these shares were worth £10 Million and that was the real reason why he had agreed to join the Club (so he said). When I spoke with him subsequently he told me that his bank in London, Coutts, had carried out an analysis of the value of SCH and its underlying assets in North Korea and in their view the company was genuine and the assets were worth the millions (indeed billions) that he was being told they were. That confirmation that somebody had looked at the position already was something of a comfort; not of course in any public way that might be relied on for the Takeover Panel;

but a comfort for us personally that SCH was not all pie in the sky.

Sven, of course, was also being told on a daily basis what the SCH shares were worth by Russell King (we all were). King was neither a director of nor a shareholder in SCH but that didn't seem to trouble Sven. To be fair, at least at that time, it didn't really trouble any of us; the issue would fall for more stringent analysis when it came to produce the certification for the Offer Document. What mattered in terms of personal comfort was that others had looked at the position before we had and thought it was OK.

Pausing there and looking at the impact of this on the parallel project at Notts County, it was of course equally important to Sven Goran Eriksson that the assets in North Korea were solid and substantial because he understood that it was from those assets that Notts County would substantially fund its regeneration towards Premiership glory; the millions to be spent in proposed transfer fees, player salaries and stadium development would come from SCH by way of funding released through its projected listing on the Stock Exchange; Sven had been told (no doubt by Russell King and Nathan Willett) that this was all going to happen within two months of his joining the Club as Director of Football. That, of course, was a ridiculous time projection. There was simply no way that any Stock Exchange listing (let alone one of the massive scale proposed for SCH) could happen that quickly; and removing the delusion that it could be was one of the initial points of dispute between me and Derek Tread (who certainly thought a two month lead time was realistic, hence his distaste for "legalese" and "red tape"). So all these factors were linked together; the solidity and worth of the SCH assets and the speed with which they could be realised on a listing underpinned not only the corporate strategy being pursued by King, Tread and Leech but it also lay at the heart of the plans that were being put in place for Notts County by the new management at Meadow Lane. A lot of the disaffection which came to light at the Club a month or so later (for example Sol Campbell's well publicized walk out) was caused by the failure of the corporate strategy to generate the millions within the very few months that Russell King thought they could be; the Club was left critically starved of cash as a result. I will come back to that later.

Of course Sven too must have been personally dissatisfied that the shares he had been offered in SCH (which he was told and believed were worth at least £10 million) also turned out to be so much scrap paper following the failure of the corporate strategy to deliver on SCH's London listing either within the timeframe that he had been told to expect or, indeed, at all. It is a wonder that he and Sol Campbell did not walk out of Meadow Lane at the same time; after two months, when no cash at all had been generated from SCH and the Club were finding it difficult to pay the milkman, Sven's goodwill must have been stretched to breaking point.

But until those cracks started to show, there is little question but that Sven Goran Eriksson had been an enthusiastic participant in what he usually called "the Project" at Notts County.

He had even been a member of the SCH Delegation which had travelled to North Korea in June 2009 for the purpose of perfecting the asset agreement with members of the North Korean presidium; the same agreement which Russell King had given me a copy of and to which I have already referred. Sven subsequently recorded his impressions of that visit (with the obvious benefit, it should be said, of twenty twenty hindsight):

"I was in the Palace and they were handing over to the North Korean Government the so-called shares.

I asked them how much that was because at the same time we couldn't pay the milk bill at Notts County and what they told me was not millions, it was billions of dollars.

They used my name. Of course they did. And at the end it was a big, big mistake".[1]

From my point of view, the fact that Sven had been part of the SCH North Korean Delegation (I was shown the photographs) added, not a lot but enough, to the credibility of the documents which Russell King had brought back with him. It was at least clear that there *had* been a meeting in Pyongyang; that it *had* included key members of the North Korean Presidium (they were in the photograph with Sven) and that SCH had been given whatever the rights were worth.

Surely nobody could make all of that up?

But returning now to the corporate narrative, and having explained why Blue Book compliance and asset valuations were of key importance to the process, my lawyers were coming back from the First London's due diligence meetings in less than high spirits, indeed with all passion spent:

---

[1] Daily Mail Interview

"Keith Brentford doesn't know what he's doing".

That sounded a little fatalistic to me:

"What do you mean?"

"I gave him our due diligence list and he told me most of the questions were irrelevant"

"So what you really mean is that Keith Brentford thinks that **you** don't know what you're doing?"

"Yes, but we do. He looks to me as though he's out of his depth."

Bearing in mind the enormity of the transaction we were contemplating that seemed to me very likely; I suspected most of us were out of our depth on a transaction of this size. Not for the first time, I wondered why they had come to a firm as small as ours. My corporate colleague seemed to be thinking the same thing:

"We can't handle this. It's too big."

She suggested that now was the time to bring in active assistance from Milbank Tweed. I agreed with her and off she went to make the call.

Almost as soon as she had left my room Keith Brentford was on the phone to me. He had obviously already spoken with Derek Tread and what he told me proved to be the exact mirror image of what I had heard only moments before:

"Your people aren't up to this. They are asking a lot of ridiculous questions".

I felt obliged to point out to Keith, not for the first time, that our client was actually SCH, not First London; so it was for us to frame the questions not him; and that with the best will in the world it wasn't really for the other party to the transaction to tell us what to do. No joy there:

"Paul, listen up……. we are all on the same side on this transaction and I don't want your team fouling it all up."

I didn't know what that even meant.

"Keith, I don't know what that means. Can you not just answer the questions or at the very least tell me why they are so ridiculous and I will talk with my people?"

"Derek isn't happy either. We may have to look at our representation here."

"But Keith, we *don't* represent you………"

And so it began and went on, in ever decreasing circles. My time would have been more productively spent teaching macramé to a dingo. But at least one profound truth did emerge from the call: "*Derek isn't happy*"; that was to become a constant refrain over the coming weeks. God was, presumably, in his heaven, or what passed for Derek Tread's heaven, but all wasn't well with his world.

It wasn't going particularly well in my world either and I'll tell you why.

Milbank Tweed

I had agreed in principle to involve Milbank Tweed in the SCH transaction because I was persuaded that we really had no other choice in the matter. As I have touched on from time to time already, that point had three components. First, that my firm was just too small to take on such an enormous transaction (I could understand that); secondly, that our small team of corporate lawyers (four in all) were all too inexperienced (this one I found more difficult to accept: why were we paying them City of London rates if they were not up to doing City of London work?); and, thirdly, to stand any chance of persuading the City Takeover Panel to approve the terms of the Offer Document, we would have to have a large law firm on board to do the asking (which I thought was just ridiculous).

But there we are; wiser heads than mine thought otherwise. I had already agreed that we should work with them on the deal; indeed, I had been persuaded that we couldn't work without them, and with the stimulus of what Keith Brentford and my colleague had just said, now was the time to secure Milbank Tweed's active involvement. We were about to get to know their people a whole lot better.

From their later billing figures it was as though Milbank Tweed had at least twenty lawyers working on the job; otherwise there would not be enough man hours in Western Europe to justify their charges; but during the course of the transaction we had regular contact with only three of them.

Their lead partner was a New Zealand lawyer called Stuart Harray. I had been told that he was undoubtedly smart enough to look after the issues which the transaction was likely to raise (I was told this, indeed, by one of our *own* corporate lawyers who had been turned down by Stuart's old firm, Allen and Overy); and it was true, Stuart certainly knew what he was talking about. If I had any issues with him they were not to do with his competence; he is an excellent lawyer, rather it was a general sense on my part that he was barely controlling his irritation that *we* were involved in the transaction at all. I got the impression from a very early stage that he would much rather have been doing all this on his own. I wish he had been. Looking back on it all now, this strikes me as deeply ironic because Stuart Harray was at such pains to ensure that his firm would look to City Law (in other words, *me*) to pay their fees rather than SCH as our common client. Unlike me, he was obviously astute enough to understand from the outset that all might not be well with Russell King and SCH and if everything fell apart he was determined to make sure that City Law would be underwriting his fees. He set about that task with an almost cynical devotion to self-preservation, presenting me on day two of the transaction with a letter of retainer which would make City Law personally responsible for his fees. I remember receiving that letter and wondering just how great the payment risk was; what if King and SCH did not pay us, or if they did not reimburse us for Milbank Tweed's fees? Could we then afford to pay them from our own resources? It was a difficult call and it wasn't helped by Stuart Harray snapping at my heels on a three hourly basis.

But as I sounded the position out for a day or so, I also was constantly told that Milbank involvement was not a matter of preference; they were indispensable. So in the end I decided to sign up to their letter so as to get the transaction underway; I felt reasonably confident that provided we had a regular (preferably weekly) snapshot of what Milbank Tweed were charging at any one time, and given this was the start of the transaction when not a lot would be happening (the initial due diligence was being substantially run by my own corporate lawyers and I intended to keep it that way as much as I could); then I felt reasonably comfortable that the cost exposure could be contained. I intended to pass the fee updates straight over to Russell King as they came in and if there was a problem, even of the slightest kind (a day's delay would be enough) I could always suspend Milbank from working so as to prevent our being on the hook for some enormous costs liability. That was the plan anyway.

So I signed the retainer letter and, for the time being at least, Stuart Harray was happy.

I could sense though that he was always straining at his leash to have a lot more to do on the transaction. I remember coming from a very early meeting and telling Stuart by text, by way of a general courtesy briefing, that there could be an issue with the regulator given SCH was taking over a London bank. So far as it went that was true, but in truth too, I knew that there were very little if any regulatory issues of any substance that would arise from the transaction (the effective emphasis in my text was on the word "could"). I would be surprised if Stuart Harray did not know that too. In fact I'm sure he did. But despite this his immediate reaction to my text was to call me repeatedly for the next two hours; and, when I eventually answered his calls (which I did if only to get rid of him for half an hour or so), he was offering me the services of a team of regulatory lawyers at Milbank Tweed to prepare a "full report" on what we both knew at base was a non-issue. Frankly, if I needed a report on any issue of regulatory law or practice I knew where to look for the lawyers in London who could produce it, and none of them were currently working at Milbank Tweed. I told Stuart Harray that as politely as I could, but the palpable falling off in enthusiasm at the other end of the line gave me the distinct impression that I was forcing a favourite rubber toy out of the jaws of an over enthusiastic Labrador.

And so it went on. What about more daily involvement from him with his corporate assistant; would that be helpful? No, it wouldn't. That would only triple the daily fee and, as I have touched on, I was keeping a wary eye on the daily legal spend as it was. What about a Milbank Tweed employment or tax lawyer? I gave him the same answer.

I found it harder to turn down Stuart Harray's request that we should schedule daily briefing calls so that he could be kept informed on what was happening across the transaction at large. Given I was being told, although to be fair by this stage I had pretty much stopped asking about alternatives, that we absolutely had no choice but to have Milbank Tweed involved, it was probably asking too much to try to get out of briefing their lead lawyer on what was happening from time to time. But I didn't want to commit myself to doing that on a daily basis; as it was I was already getting pretty much sick of either fending off calls from Stuart Harray or, still worse, actually having to speak with him. Some form of controlled regular briefing was probably for the best if only to moderate my exposure to him effectively. But there was no way I was going to agree to do that on the daily basis which Stuart Harray had suggested. That would be more than the human frame could bear. I suggested that we speak every Monday, Wednesday and Friday instead and to his credit he agreed.

It was suggested to me by one of our people at the time that this every second day briefing would be used as a vehicle by Milbank Tweed to run up fees; invoice items that would read suspiciously thinly like *"considering issues arising out of Monday's briefing."* Well, I frankly doubted they would do that and still do. Stuart Harray suffered from an excess of zeal and unrestrained enthusiasm but I didn't think Milbanks would do that,

But, where were we? I said there were three members of the Milbank Tweed team who we were introduced to on any regular basis; and indeed there were.

The second of them, in order of seniority, was a corporate assistant to Stuart Harray who, we were told, was a "Blue Book expert". As if to prove his expertise, he had turned up to our first meeting with an actual copy of the Blue Book; studded with yellow post it notes. Now I had been told several years earlier by a very eminent QC (specialising in corporate law as it happens) that if you don't have time to prepare for a meeting properly the thing to do is to litter the file or books you bring with you with dozens of post it notes; and if possible to annotate a few of them with beguiling cross references. So this young fellow from Milbank with his Blue Book under his arm wasn't fooling anyone, least of all me. It was though quite exciting to see an actual copy of the book close up.

I was told that he had only just joined Milbank Tweed; in fact that he hadn't even joined them yet; he was formally scheduled to start only in a months' time. But Milbank Tweed had accelerated his start date especially so that he would be able to join the team on the SCH transaction. In retrospect that should have been a warning sign; it suggested Milbank Tweed did not in fact have any other lawyers at his level who were experienced in Blue Book work of this kind; why else assign us a lawyer who had not even started with them? That point escaped me at the time. What didn't escape me though was the arch comment that one of our own corporate lawyers made: why are they calling him in early if there is enough work for him to do otherwise at Milbank Tweed? It was almost as though, without the SCH transaction, there would be nothing else for him to do when he joined. I thought that was a pretty good point, but amidst the background noise of constantly being told that Milbanks were indispensable, I let it go.

He was, to be sure, a very pleasant young man. It would have taken a Body Shop shelf of sponges to soak up the wetness behind his ears, but he was a very pleasant young man. Understandably, he spent his time during our meetings raising a series of points relevant to the operation of the City Takeover Code. That was what he was being paid to do after all; and the points he made were certainly good enough in themselves, indeed, for the most part, they were crucial to the success of the transaction; but somehow they invariably worked always to inflame Derek Tread's thinly restrained temper.

At least during the course of my dealings with him as part of these various transactions, Derek Tread seemed unnaturally predisposed to treat any legal intervention as part of an unspoken conspiracy amongst lawyers to block or slow down his beloved deals; so one can readily imagine the effect on his blood pressure of the following typical question from our man at Milbank Tweed:

"Can we just take a look at issues of standing and fitness for the directors, who will be dealing with that? The City Takeover…….."

"What do you mean?"

"Well, whether the individuals are fit and proper to be involved in the management of First London, which is a regulated…………"

"What the *fuck* does ***that*** mean!"

Tread's face had gone from ghostly white to blast furnace red in a nanosecond; the table instantly quietened in fear.

"Well, we obviously don't want to make too much of this Derek…….but we are required to deal with

85

the standing of the individuals in question; whether they are fit and proper to be involved in the management of a regulated entity. That is dealt with in the City Takeover………..”

"I don't give a *fuck* about that; are you saying that anyone here is **not** fit and proper to be involved in the management….. We are all in this deal together; we're on the same side, what it…..the management of a public company is. Because if you are, tell me now rather than bottling it up. I'm sick of all this legalese…………..”

He scanned his line of otherwise bored colleagues (they had obviously heard this act before at a hundred other meetings):

"…….I'm just sick that's all, of all this legalese and red tape……for *God's* sake.

He threw his eyes up to the ceiling at this last (frankly blasphemous) comment and slunk back in his chair.

"No, I'm not saying that Derek……. I'm not saying that Derek, it's just that we need to look at the point………"

Unlike him, I *would* have said it. Kevin Leech for one, and best friend that he was; I would say that as Jersey's record bankrupt, he was then at least unfit to be involved in the management of a regulated financial institution; and Russell King, knowing what I know now, definitely; but even then, Russell King was colourably unfit to have anything to do with the transaction. Those two for one and I was reserving judgement on the rest of them round the table.

But I said nothing. Not then anyway.

Milbank man clearly hoped to rescue himself by changing the subject; at least a little by drilling further into the detail (as I am sure he himself would have put it) but if anything he only succeeded in making an already bad situation worse:

"Perhaps we could drill into the detail…..

87

(I told you so)

"……….drill into the detail a bit more; that might help us to get a better handle on the issue. Can we take a look at who actually controls these various companies, starting with Swiss Commodity Holding; let's take a look at that, which are the individuals or entities who have a material interest in controlling Swiss Commodity Holding?"

"What do you mean?"

Derek Tread's comment, which was if anything getting to be as much a habit as his throwing his eyes up to the ceiling, was of course utterly fatuous; but I was interested in hearing the answer. Who exactly *did* control Swiss Commodity Holding?

I held my pencil at the ready.

Another silence took hold around the table; broken by Derek Tread again:

"What the *fuck* does that mean?

Those of us who weren't as adept at dealing daily with Derek Tread (that was pretty much all of us around the table) gave a little involuntary jump as he barked "*fuck*".

"Well, Derek; the City Takeover Code…….."

"I don't give a *fuck* about that. I'm sick of all this legalese………."

And so it went on. You get the picture.

I'm not sure whether Derek Tread broke the young man's spirit; perhaps he did, but over the weeks that followed we saw less and less of him. I wouldn't blame him if he had formed the view that discretion was the better part of valour; and chose for a couple of weeks anyway, to take part in further meetings by way of telephone only. That way at least there was less chance of his being punched by his client and he could always, in the last resort, claim that the line had gone dead and go off and find a pub.

With the best will in the world, these kind of exchanges and these kinds of meetings could not go on forever; they were just too acidic and too inconclusive; and after a while they were doing nothing more than reinforcing the feeling, at least for me but maybe for others as well, that this was all really a bit bonkers. Given we were not able to involve ourselves in the transaction without participation from Milbank Tweed, I had been told that often enough, and given Derek Tread obviously hated the chosen representative of Milbank Tweed (he hadn't even met Stuart Harray), things could only go one of two ways. Either the young man from Milbank would go mad and retire of his own accord or the client would tell us to get rid of him.

I waited to see which of the two it was to be.

Happily for our young fellow from Milbank Tweed, it was the getting rid of option; and the word, when it came, came not only from Derek Tread but from Russell King and Nathan Willett as well. Within a single two day period all three of them asked me to get rid of Milbank Tweed; not of course in a Mafia sense, even in the City of London things are still a lot more civilised than that. Derek Tread told me that Milbank Tweed were "useless" and I had to sack them; I pointed out, not for the first time. that Tread was not actually my client and neither was First London; but, not for the first time either, this seemed hardly to dilute the force of his instructions at all, indeed it seemed to reinforce his resolve which had become venomous: "*Just talk to Russell Paul, but get rid of them; they doesn't know what they're doing, nobody at Milbank does, and we are all sick and tired of all this legalese.*" Willett called me literally within ten minutes of Tread and made the same points; virtually in the same words (it was almost as though they had scripted each other for the call), he too was sick of all this legalese .....Apparently. But he wasn't my client either. I needed instructions from someone at SCH and that meant the big fat heap of wobbling agency that was Russell King. I waited for him to call as well because I was sure that he would. This was something of an unholy trinity.

But unlike his chums, Russell King didn't call me that day. He only managed to wobble onto the phone the day after and then only in response to an e-mail I had sent him on the evening of the previous day when I had spoken with Derek Tread and Nathan Willett.

I put had put together a pretty terse e-mail that evening to send to Russell King, reporting on what Tread and Willett had said and setting out my views as to Milbank Tweed's proposed sacking; but what obviously attracted Russell King's attention (as indeed it had mine) was the attachment to that e-mail which was the cost "snapshot" that I had received from Milbank Tweed the same evening.

Now, to make sense of what follows you have to bear in mind that by this stage of the SCH transaction, since, that is, the original meeting which I had with Russell King and his mates at the Dorchester, we had been working on the deal for about three weeks in all.

Milbank Tweed had been actively involved for about two and a half weeks and I had signed our fee letter with Stuart Harray some two weeks earlier. In that two weeks, Derek Tread had beaten their blue book man into submission and I had converted Stuart Harray's offers of help into three times a week telephone briefings which, for the reasons I have already explained, I was intent on keeping as short and uninformative as possible (to avoid having further help thrust upon me, certainly, but also because, in general, life was just too short to listen to Stuart Harry with anything like that kind of frequency on anything like a sustained basis).

So, when their sacking was looking imminent, as it obviously was following my conversations with Derek Tread and Nathan Willett, I thought this was probably a good time to find out what Milbank Tweed had on the clock by way of fees. With their usual admirable efficiency, I had received that within an hour or so of asking for the breakdown; and now that I had it, I thought we were unlikely to need Milbank Tweed again, not after Russell King had seen what they were proposing to charge for two and a half week's work.

£92,000.

After seeing this I had half a mind to sack them myself but Russell King saved me the trouble by demanding, that is not too light a word for it, *demanding* that we suspend Milbank Tweed's retainer with immediate effect by reason of being, in his view (where he was at least at one with Tread and Willett) all round useless; but also because they were, as he also put it to me during the call, "taking the piss". I didn't necessarily agree with that; not then, and I wouldn't say so even now. Taking the piss is obviously a mortal sin, I see that obviously; but Milbank Tweed were only doing their job, and doing it indeed under very difficult circumstances.

Having said that, I am pretty sure that these instructions were just about the single most sensible thing that Russell King had asked me to do during the entire period of the two month's mad hatter's tea party that he presided over; there again, this wasn't exactly setting the bar particularly high bearing in mind that almost everything else that he said to me or asked me to do during this period was utterly stupid.

Anyway, loyal to my instructions and my client, I fired off an immediate e-mail to Stuart Harray. His retainer was suspended with immediate effect.
He was on the phone to me in a heartbeat. What could he possibly have done wrong to deserve *this*?

Although it was difficult, at least in immediate terms, to resist a warm sense of wellbeing at the thought of not having to endure any more Milbank Tweed briefing calls, there was also of course a pang of unease. My firm was responsible for these fees; I had rashly assumed that Milbank Tweed's ability to rack up fees would be limited through a combination of the part we were playing on the transaction and the fairly limited to time that we had been working together: it should have been possible to limit their fees by saying "no", for example, to the various service suggestions that Stuart Harray had been dunning me with during the past two weeks; which, to be fair, is exactly what I had thought I had been doing. Could it be possible that even so the time spent by Milbank Tweed's wet eared young man in going head to head with Derek Tread could actually justify a fee of £92,000?

Balancing that unease, I was still very conscious of Milbank Tweed's supposed indispensability on the transactions. I doubted that everybody I had spoken to could be wrong on that; they were good lawyers and whatever Derek Tread and Russell king might think, they had added real value to the documents during the short time that we had been working together. Anyway, now wasn't the time to rock the boat in case they had to come back in again later (which indeed they did) so I wasn't about to piss them off gratuitously by passing on what both Tread and King had told me verbatim.

I shared the figure we had been given by Milbanks for their fees with some of our own people; they all expressed astonishment and muttered darkly of SCH being milked The language they actually used was, in fact, slightly harsher and rather more earthy than that but I will spare it here. I didn't necessarily agree with that though; and here's why.

The figure was high; of course it was, indeed in some ways nose bleedingly high, but it wasn't as though I hadn't seen the like of this before. I had. I remember in one of the previous law firms that I had worked with (Lovells) being asked to put together a budget for the liquidators of the failed BCCI when they were about to bring their claim against the Bank of England for failing to spot that BCCI had been raddled with fraud from top to bottom for years. One would have thought that those in charge at BCCI could have worked that out for themselves without relying on the sleepy headed Cerberus of Threadneedle Street. Anyway, back to the budget; on that occasion I had tried to construct a line by line costs projection for the client based primarily on the size of the legal team that we had put together for the litigation plus the (six) barristers that we would need from time to time and based on the assumption (not unreasonable I thought) that each member of the team would be working a seven hour day on the case for four years (half that for the barristers because they have longer lunches); that came out with a bottom line figure for the whole action of some £4 million. I thought that was quite a lot of money to spend on a piece of litigation; I still do, you could buy most of Rotherham for that. But no, it was a serious understatement of the spend if anything, according to the partner I was working for and who was in charge of the litigation; he told me blithely that the case would cost £250,000 a fortnight and there weren't enough hours in the day to get to that number on the basis of the formula I had used. He was at least right about that; there weren't enough hours in the day. He explained that it was a question of *headline expectations*, not just adding up the actual *work done* by the relevant lawyers and other fee earners.

The partner in question was a fellow called Christopher Grierson; I worked with him quite a lot when I was at Lovells and he was quite well known in his field of financial crime and white collar fraud; which is itself ironic because Christopher was later found guilty of three charges of fraud involving nefarious abstractions from Lovell's' office accounts in excess of £1.2 Million (just shy of five weeks work on the BCCI claim in case you are trying to work it out); he was sentenced to three years in prison in May 2012. As best I know that had nothing whatsoever to do with his earlier generic approach to litigation budgeting. In fact, according to the report in the Daily Mail, it had more to do with his obsession for a young Lebanese lady in New York on whom he lavished over £600,000 over an 18 month period. Who knows the secrets of the human heart eh? Poor old Christopher.

Of course I am not suggesting any such shenanigans on the part of anyone from the Milbank Tweed team on our SCH transaction. Not at all; all three of them were and are very honest and trustworthy. No, there was no suggestion of Grierson goings on here. Only a mild unease on my part that in the immediate aftermath of the biggest financial crash in living memory (which had happened in 2008 in case you need reminding, the year before the SCH transaction was starting up), the London office of an American Law Firm might not have enough work to do and might be doing it in our office instead.

But you get the point; I knew that law firms, especially those with their snouts in the square mile troughs, could well charge something in the order of £100,000 for two weeks work whatever the rest of the world might think about the obscenity of such a figure. The BCCI budget spend was *double* that. I remember also working for Mirror Group Newspapers (again when I was a young lawyer at Lovells); this was to do with the millions upon millions that Robert Maxwell had plundered from the Mirror Group Pension Scheme so as to shore up his collapsing business empire. We had the rash idea of putting in an accountant to act as court appointed receiver over Robert Maxwell's estate (Maxwell had committed suicide when the fact of the frauds came to light, he dropped over the side of his yacht in the midnight hour); we did that just in case there were assets there which could be used later to satisfy Mirror Group's claims (there weren't in fact, Maxwell had very little left beyond his interest in Oxford City Football Club – football again). Anyway, we chose to appoint a partner in a firm of accountants to act as receiver but, wary of the fees again, we told him that the client would need to be told once he had incurred costs of £50,000. This was in 1991 when £50,000 was £50,000. I was very surprised to receive a phone call less than one week later telling me that the receiver had hit the threshold spend. *Less than a week*! As with Milbanks eighteen years later, his retainer was suspended too; but in his case, unlike Milbanks, he just carried on acting anyway as he was a court appointed receiver; he carried on acting in fact until every last penny in value in the estate had been soaked up and used to pay his fees and when there was nothing left he stopped; when there was no more money he decided to resign his office and go and look elsewhere for plunder. For that little exercise in avarice he was hauled before the Social Services Select Committee by Frank Field MP and accused of "bayonetting the dead". As with so much else he said and did over the years, Frank Field was bang on the money there.

So yes, I knew that using a firm of accountants or lawyers in the City of London could cost a lot of money very quickly. So I had no particular reason to accuse Milbanks of overstating their costs in any way; even though I was clearly worried that I might end up having to pay them. That was the real cause of concern.

More than the actual figure itself, more or less for the first time at least in any sustained way, my concern was now whether Swiss Commodity Holding would actually cough up the funds we would need to cover these costs. It was, of course, very far from fanciful to predict that we would soon be required to pay Milbanks the thick end of £100,000 from our own coffers whether SCH paid us or not. All those questions about the standing of SCH and who actually owned SCH were starting to acquire an enhanced resonance. Not panic bells as yet; not at that stage at least, but definitely a niggling sense of unease as to what might lie down the road on these transactions.

Just stopping Milbanks from charging us more than the £92,000 they already had was not altogether an answer. They *had* already charged us £92,000 and we had only been instructed in these transactions for a little over a month so far. None of our fees had been paid. It was ridiculous to contemplate but the situation was so unusual and asymmetric, so out of the ordinary, that it almost felt as though the more we did for these clients and the longer we were involved in these transactions, the more it was going to cost us. Lawyers usually act for clients in the expectation that they will make money, not lose it; particularly in transactions with the scale these ones had.

All things considered, I was not particularly happy with the situation; it was too edgy for my liking. It was not simply the scale of the thing; I had been involved in very large scale work before, such as the liquidation of BCCI and the Mirror Pension fund litigation arising out of Robert Maxwell's record breaking frauds; no, it wasn't the scale of the thing, it was the almost ethereal sense of unreality which was making it difficult to find concrete answers to what were proving to be almost impressionistic problems. It was difficult to pin anything solid down. So however edgy the whole thing felt, and it certainly *did* feel edgy, ultimately it seemed best to me simply to suspend work on the Milbank side, hold the ring and carry on with the transaction without them as best as we could; wait and see what would come up over the coming weeks rather than withdraw from the matter altogether. But I was intent more than ever now on pressing Russell King to be more explicit as to just exactly who was in charge at SCH; and, indeed, on just when we could expect to be paid. I put together our first invoice for SCH shortly after I had finished speaking with Russell King that afternoon and in case you were wondering, no; they never paid it.

In terms of my ongoing relationship with Russell King and the rest of his cohorts, it wasn't exactly the end of the beginning but it was certainly the beginning of the end.

I mentioned earlier, as you may remember, that there were *three* lawyers we got to know at Milbank Tweed during the course of the SCH transaction. Well, the third was Russell Jacobs who was, at least at the time (I don't know what he's doing now), their managing partner in London. Russell was to become involved later on and as a result of the combustible combination of our decision not to take Milbank Tweed to task on the level of their fees at an early enough stage and a quirky proclivity of Russell King to keep going back to Milbank Tweed for help after they had been "sacked"; he asked for their help subsequently in connection with the purchase of the BMW Sauber Formula One Racing Team which was hardly an insignificant matter. If nothing else this demonstrated his inherent diffidence to the Milbank retainer: however often he told me Milbanks were, in his view, "useless" he still went back to them whenever he needed the scale services which only a firm of their size could offer. He was like a child with brain freeze; he couldn't wait to get his next ice lolly. He lived entirely in his fat, bloated moments.

Russell Jacobs later dealt with good grace and as best he could with the politics and economic meltdown arising from his firm not being paid at all. That, though, is another story for another day.

For now, we ought to take a look at what was going on at Notts County while all these complicated, Blue Book related corporate type things were happening. The temporary failure of SCH's corporate strategy to produce a tide of money within the two month period that Sven Goran Eriksson, for one, had been led to expect (he wasn't alone in that, Tread and King had expected a two month flood as well); the failure of SCH to secure its expected funding within two months was having a radical and progressively catastrophic effect on the financial standing of the Football Club. I have touched earlier on Sven Goran Eriksson's subsequent interview with the *Daily Mail* (given with the full benefit of hindsight) where he talked about the Club not being able to pay its milk bill, and it was at this time, when the planned takeover of First London was starting to founder, that the cash squeeze was starting to show most obviously for the first time; the Club was gradually being starved of cash, to such an extent that its very existence was ultimately threatened; and this, remember, was the oldest football league club in the world.

The Litigation Circus

A couple of days after my first meeting with him at the Dorchester, Russell King called me again from his Suite (at least that's where he said he was).

"I have another little job for you".

I waited with bated breath. What could it be this time?

"We need you to throw the Rugby Club out of Meadow Lane. They are churning up the pitch and anyway, we don't want them in here. Can you look after that?"

I never liked Rugby. Being a State School lad it had, for me, far too much of the ambience of Deep Heat as well as the unwholesome prospect of ominously close contact with another boy's inner thighs. There was no love lost between me and the rugby fraternity:

"No problem; send us over the documentation and we'll take a look at it. I won't though be able to look after this one personally; I'm too busy. Will you be happy if I have my Partner, Helen Mulcahy, look after this one?"

That last bit was substantially true but I also had an eye to the fact that Helen Mulcahy, with whom I had founded the Firm three years earlier, had no real work to do; she attracted little if anything by way of new instructions and in general spent most of her day ordering pencils over the internet and wine for the office fridge. Even for her, that was not the best use of her time.

"Sure, I'd like to work with her."

That was a result. I had killed three birds with one stone: a counter blast to the rugby fraternity which I disliked from birth; a new instruction for my firm and so some money for me (hopefully) and some much needed work for Helen Mulcahy (the third of the three birds). It was all very satisfactory.

I arranged for King to speak with Helen Mulcahy and from that moment onwards she became the point person at the firm for the day to day work that was carried out on behalf of Notts County over the next two months. As she had so very little to do otherwise, Helen Mulcahy was very careful to hoard the little work she did have to herself. She was incredibly selective in telling me what she was getting up to on behalf of the Club. As she volunteered virtually nothing to my in the beaten path of conversation, I had to prise the little information that I could out of her like monkey nuts out of a shell. It could be hard work. She jealously guarded her contacts with Russell King and the Club with a particular ferocity and would willingly involve me with what was going on only when some disaster was looming (more of that later). Otherwise she would only drop snippets of information to me; and even then, for the most part, only when she was talking to someone else in the office and I happened to be standing nearby. But having said that a lot of the drops and drippings were, to be fair to her, of an unusually high quality.

For example, it was from Helen Mulcahy that I found out that Sven Goran Erickson was planning to sign David Beckham to Notts County and that the drafting of a new contract for him to join the Club was at a relatively advanced stage. I was surprised about that; bearing in mind its news potential I was especially surprised that she had not told me about it earlier, characteristically I heard about the signing only as part of a throwaway line during the course of a call I made to her from South Africa (to talk about something else entirely): "*oh, nothing much, we should be signing David Beckham to Notts County next week.......*"; that sort of thing. Then silence. It was like pulling teeth:

"When do you think you will be signing formally; is the Club planning to make an announcement?"

"Oh, I don't know. Why do you want to know?"

"It may affect the Firm."

"How so?"

"You don't think it might be newsworthy; something we should look to make a press release on?"

"No. I don't like press releases."

"OK, it's up to you".

It was an unusually diffident attitude for a lawyer to take. In some ways, I suppose, it was an admirable attitude. We have grown so accustomed now to seeing wretched, oily haired solicitors advertising on daytime television for volunteers to come forward who have fallen off a ladder in the last three years; sometimes they will call up and leave messages about PPI (on the hour every half hour) and whenever there is tragedy or despair, the lawyer will be there with the name of his or her firm plastered behind them on a folding set of screens (for re-use on another occasion). But Helen Mulcahy wasn't like that. Despite the obvious newsworthy potential of what was happening at Meadow Lane, she didn't seem to want to sully her hands with the yellow press; maybe she had a premonition that the *Sun* were about to fuck her beloved Russell over (as indeed it was; *that* was one of those crises when she *did* want me to help and let me know what was happening).

For the time being though I just asked her to keep me posted on developments.

I remember when Helen Mulcahy was much younger and she had just started working for me at an earlier firm; as she had been working at that firm for several months without a valid visa from the Home Office[2] we had to send her off for a couple of months to travel around Europe before applying properly to re-enter the country with valid documents. That, of course, was not especially great publicity for a law firm

---

[2] Helen Mulcahy is Australian.

which had been routinely offering advice to the unsuspecting public on immigration issues; it didn't say much that it couldn't get things organised properly (let alone legally) for its own members of staff. I had arranged for Helen to spend a few weeks in Monte Carlo where one of my clients had documents that needed to be reviewed; because I didn't want her to spend her whole time away hanging around doing nothing, which was something she would get a lot better at doing later on. The point being that she was twenty seven years old or so at that time and we had arranged to bring her back business class on the flight home from Nice; on the trip back she sat next to David Beckham and Posh Spice who were coming home from their honeymoon. She was as skittish and excited as a schoolgirl. She told the Beckham- Spices that I was a Manchester United Fan (Beckham played for United then) and asked for and came away with their autographs for me, barely able to breathe as she handed them to me back in London; even a day later her heart was still pounding at her brush with fame. Maybe that is what made her so publicity shy; the memory of that and in some way a feeling that she would treat David Beckham as she might any old cleaner or typist signing up for a contract at the Club.

On a more serious note and during the course of the same call from South Africa (something of a triumph for inter partner communication at City Law Helen Mulcahy also told me that Notts County had signed Kasper Schmeichel as its goalkeeper; that had happened after the transfer deadline so, as part of its compliance procedures with the Football League (the Club's Regulator), Mulcahy had been required to swear an affidavit confirming that Notts County had the financial standing to meet its ongoing commitments over the course of the coming season. When she told me about that, my ears immediately pricked up; I was still, for one thing, waiting for SCH to pay our bill and doubts had started to circulate in my mind as to Russell King's standing (for the reasons set out at the end of the last chapter). What had she said in her affidavit? Anything to do with the solvency or financial viability of the companies which lay behind the acquisition of the Football Club would be of key importance to us; she told me, in answer, that she had signed up to a sworn statement of the Club's solvency and financial viability having been shown a copy of a "guarantee" which the Club's owner (Blenheim) had received from First London.

I asked to see a copy of the guarantee as soon as I got back to London.

It is fair to say that Helen Mulcahy knew very little about technical banking matters but her lack of any inquiring instinct on the First London guarantee verged on staggering. It had been worded so that First London would make funds available to Blenheim; but only up to a limit of £5 Million (very little in the context of its seemingly limitless expansion plans) and then only to the extent that a creditor had first secured a court judgement against the Club, and even then only if the judgement had gone unsatisfied following execution. I had never seen a guarantee in those terms before; it was ridiculous. By way of only one example, the guarantee could not be called on to meet a tax bill, but if the Inland Revenue put the club into liquidation and got nothing out of the liquidation to satisfy the same tax bill *then* it could be called on; but by then, of course, the Club would for all practical purposes have ceased to exist. It also looked to be uncomfortably discretionary, so that if First London decided not to pay up after all then it didn't have to. This "guarantee" wasn't worth the paper it was cobbled together on. Certainly it was not an assurance of ongoing solvency. The document was to be described in the press later in the year, by the Guardian in fact, as "unorthodox"; that was something of an understatement. It was, for all practical purposes utterly worthless.

Once I had seen the terms in which this "guarantee" had been framed it was obvious to me that Helen Mulcahy had been especially imprudent in relying on it for the purpose of giving the declaration of solvency required by the Football League. It had no financial significance one way or the other; it was, as I have said, utterly worthless. The key question was where the Club was deriving its capital funding from for its ongoing spending because it sure as hell wasn't getting anything from Munto in the British Virgin Islands (which owned Blenheim, the operating company which in turn owned the Club); neither was it getting funds from any of the other SCH entities, all of which were very recently incorporated shelf companies whose capital funding was across the board dependant on a rapid Stock Exchange Listing for SCH which (see above) wasn't happening any time soon and certainly not within the timeframes that those involved in the management of the Club had been led to expect.

In those circumstances the Club was running entirely off its (limited) income generating powers (gate receipts, shop and sponsorship for the most part); and that was never going to be enough to cover the major spending that the management had embarked on; Kasper Schmeichel for one, Sol Campbell for another. Sooner or later it wouldn't even be able to pay the milk bill. But of course nobody was coming clean at the Club about the delays and difficulties on the SCH listing. So this major spending program was simply never reined back in time. In that context, even if the

First London Guarantee hadn't been useless (which it was) it was undoubtedly a commercial irrelevance. It said nothing whatsoever about the Club's solvency and financial standing.

There was little doubt but that Sven's very public involvement as Director of Football at Notts County was sufficient even so to add a veneer of respectability and credibility to the whole operation as it spiralled downhill under this unsupported cycle of debt. No doubt that is exactly what Russell King had in mind when he brought Sven on board.

And Sven had certainly captured the media's attention. The talk in that Summer of 2009, just as the new football season was about to start, was dominated by speculation on whether Notts County was destined for a rapid rise through the league system; right through to the riches of the Premier League. Many well respected commentators were saying that it would do just that, and do it, moreover, in three successive seasons; as proof of their intent they pointed not only to Eriksson's involvement (he was, after all, a former manager of the England International team and had a glittering club record (including most recently at Manchester City) but, ironically, they pointed also to the very spending spree which was placing the Club's future in jeopardy.

I placed a £20 bet on Notts County myself; I bet on them making it to the Premiership by 2012. I don't know where that betting slip is now; otherwise I might be tempted to frame it.

Helen Mulcahy appeared on the BBC's *Football League Show*; accompanied by Sven-Goran Erickson and Nathan Willett, taking her seat before the game (a game which County prophetically lost 1-0). She arrived like an over excited schoolgirl in the office on Monday morning to make us all watch the programme on BBC's i Player. She seemed quite at home in the company of King and Willett; and well she might, because by now she was also going great guns with the Club's batch of new litigation.

There is a saying in legal circles: *there are no fleas on a dead dog.* Meaning that one of the signs of life in any commercial organisation is the presence of continuing low level litigation; on this hypothesis any company ought to look to be in court fairly regularly, either fighting off claims or bringing them to demonstrate to the world that it is in active good health. By reference to that benchmark at least, if none of the usual benchmarks, the Football Club was in buoyant good health. It was suing and being sued by everyone in sight. Helen Mulcahy was everywhere. First, of course, and as presaged by my earlier conversation with Russell King, it had sued the Rugby Club with which it shared its ground at Meadow Lane. As King had told me, the Rugby players were churning up the pitch so there was no way a High Court Judge could fail to deliver a judgement ejecting them from the Stadium. But he did. This first outing in Court was, in other words, an abject failure; and Helen Mulcahy returned to the office full of tales of public school "anti-soccer" bias. But she still lost. In rapid succession she lost the next case the Club was involved in too. Under Willett's direction, Notts County had summarily cancelled its existing sponsorship arrangements and entered instead into a new sponsorship deal with SCH which duly had its corporate emblem added to Notts County's Club Badge; their logo was an especially crass working of the letters of its name which looked somehow Orwellian on the older, faintly mediaeval symbols of the existing badge. As was inevitable, the previous and now spurned, sponsors immediately threatened litigation; they had stood by the Club for years when its average attendance was 1000 and a dog, only to find their name being airbrushed out of the records at the very time when the Club was attracting unprecedented media attention. Nothing could have been more predictable than that they should reach for a writ. The Club caved in and paid substantial damages but only after dancing the legal hornpipe long enough to enrich a few more lawyers. But that seemed not to matter, if there was a court fight to be picked, Notts County were there. It was a good job for the Club that Russell King wasn't either paying or planning to pay our fees for these little, luxury excursions (but, of course, we didn't know that at the time); lucky for the Club and Russell King given half our lawyers were assigned to his litigation at any one time.

A very fat man in the Sun

On 26 September 2009 the Sun Newspaper printed a front page story that Russell King had served a two year term in prison for insurance fraud. This came as a shuddering reality check after the weeks of media endorsement of the Project at Meadow Lane; if the story was right then Russell King was manifestly not a fit and proper person to be involved in the operation of a regulated football club; he could not possibly then pass the fitness and propriety test operated by the Football League and that would preclude him not only from being a Board Member at the Club or its Controlling Entities (which to be fair he wasn't) but also from being involved in any more indirect way in its day to day operations (which he undoubtedly was).

It was a threshold moment in many ways. Up until that point, nothing had moved or been decided at

Notts County without Russell King's say so; but if he was not fit and proper, in the way suggested by the Sun or indeed otherwise but that specifically for the time being, then things were going to have to change at Meadow Lane and change pretty quickly.

The lawyer's natural response to a story of this kind has two strategic elements. First of all, the offending publication needs to be persuaded to retract its story if at all possible and in trying to do that it is usually necessary to make dark threats of a libel action. If that doesn't work, and this is the second element, it may then actually be necessary to sue for libel to address the reputational harm (if the client is prepared to put up with the anguish and cost). In this case, of course, the story had been run by the Sun and the Sun is part of the News International stable of publications; it has teams of lawyers of its own as well as a clutch of grizzled old journalists who are better versed in these matters than the average lawyer is; they are well used to testing their own stories and are not about to retract a single syllable of them unless it can be shown *beyond question* that what the newspaper has printed is untrue. That is a steep task.

For my part, and for those reasons, I wasn't about to start threatening a libel action in this case, let alone actually start one, without knowing first that what the Sun had printed about Russell King was, *beyond question*, untrue. So the immediate urgent requirement in that light was to test what the story in the Sun had said rigorously and stringently against King's own version of events. I arranged a conference call with him that morning (within an hour or so of being told about the story) with the intention of taking a statement from King before deciding what to do next. Bear in mind that this man had been running a regulated football club, had a half interest in a London Bank and was orchestrating a £163 million corporate takeover. So, what followed was, to say the least, disconcerting.

He, of course, had already read the story. He was frothing sound and fury and court actions and public recrimination and public ingratitude; but I gradually brought him to the meat of the allegations:

"It says here Russell that you were involved in an insurance fraud; that you hid two cars, one of them an Aston Martin, in your garage in Jersey and then you put in an insurance claim saying that they had been stolen. Now, Russell, is any of that true?"

"Actually both of the cars were Aston Martins."

"OK. They were both Aston Martins. Did you tell your insurers that they had been stolen?"

"No."

"OK. So the story is false when it says that you told the insurers the cars were stolen, when they were actually in your garage at home all the time?"

There was a confident ring to my question. In my mind I was already starting to draft the e-mail which *the Sun* would be receiving thirty minutes later.

"Yes, that story is false".

There was then an uncomfortable pause:

"What do you mean *that* story Russell? Is any of *this* story true?"

"Which story are you talking about Paul? I'm really confused here".

He's confused; *he's* confused:

"I'm looking at the story on the front page of this morning's edition of *the Sun* Russell. The one we were talking about a minute ago; the one *you* are in. Is *that* story true or not?

"Oh, I see. But you were asking me, I thought, whether I had submitted a claim to my insurers for one of the Aston Martins; I told you that in fact both of the vehicles were Aston Martins so the

126

story is definitely wrong there. You understand that?"

I had obviously come across this kind of thing before; this was a client who throws up so much smoke and dust that it is virtually impossible, even for his own lawyer, to keep track of what is being said; let alone whether what is being said is actually true. I decided to deconstruct what he was saying into simple components so as to try to get a better understanding; and I also sent my assistant out to collect a tape recorder with which I could record the conversation (something told me he might misremember later what he was telling me now). I wasn't about to go on with a national newspaper without a clear record of exactly what King was saying. So I asked him to bear with us a minute, which he did; quietly and with what passed for good grace. Of course I did not tell him that the call was going to be recorded once we resumed.

I consulted my notes and started again:

"Right, we're back with you now Russell; sorry about that. You were saying, I think, that there were two Aston Martins and not one. Is that right Russell?"

"Yes, that's right."

"So the story in that respect, to the extent the story states that there was one Aston Martin rather than two; that story is untrue".

"Yes. There were two Aston Martins. Not one. That was definitely the case…there were two of them"

"OK. I've got that Russell. I'm not sure it is a decisive issue to the story but thank you for clarifying it. Then, moving on, you definitely did not submit a claim to your insurers saying that the cars were stolen."

"Correct. I didn't do that."

"Thank you; and that means neither of the cars, Russell, because *both* of the cars were all the time in your garage at home in Jersey as I understand the position. Is that right?"

I placed a hard emphasis on the word "***both***" and checked the recorder was still working; it was and it picked up what he said next:

"Correct."

"Well, if you never made a claim to your insurers in respect of either car Russell, then I just don't see why it matters where the cars, either of them, actually were at the time; whether in your garage or anywhere else."

"Exactly……. That's *exactly* the point Paul"

"So that means this stuff about you being sent to prison for insurance fraud just can't be right Russell. We can get a retraction on that and fix it up. What I think we should do is cut to the chase and get a Criminal Records Report today which we can send to the Sun to show their story is wrong. We won't need to enter into a process of persuasion with them then. It will all be there is black and white and we can send that on to the Football League as well, and for that matter, the City Takeover Panel to set all their minds at rest."

That wasn't overkill. I knew that the Takeover Panel would be asking questions as well because Russell King was also subject to their own fitness and propriety tests as a relevant individual on the SCH Takeover.

"We'll need your written consent to run the search Russell. I will send you over a form to sign and send back to me now".

There was a pause on his end of the line which, correctly, signalled to me that all was not going as well as it seemed to be:

"Well, I have been in Prison Paul".

Ah.

"Ah, I see. OK. What were you convicted of?"

"Insurance fraud".

"*Insurance fraud ?*"

That was a coincidence. I wondered for a second whether the Sun knew about this other offence; was there another story on the way?

"Yes, I'm afraid so Paul. I have been a bad boy".

"Can you tell me what that was all about then Russell? Obviously people, the Football League and the Takeover Panel, will need to be told about that so that we can try to make them as comfortable as possible".

I knew there wasn't a cat in hell's chance of persuading either the Football League or the City

Takeover Panel that a convicted fraudster could, in any circumstances, be a fit and proper person to run a football Club or any publicly listed company. But I might as well find out what this was all about. For his part, Russell King was still plainly animated by an aggressive optimism, the sort of optimism that must regularly have fuelled his futile court battles at Notts County; it was very hard at this stage to avoid starting to dislike him:

"That would be good Paul. It's got nothing to do with these aresholes anyway."

"So what exactly was the conviction for Russell?"

"Those two Aston Martins, I made a claim that they were stolen and then the police found that they were in my garage at home all the time. I got two years."

"But Russell, you just told me that you didn't make a claim to your insurers in relation to those two cars; the two Aston Martins. Have I misunderstood you?"

I checked that the recorder was still running.

"No. You asked me if I made a claim to my insurers."

There was more than a hint of indignation in his tone; as though I were accusing him of having been stringing me along, which in fact I think is exactly what he was trying to accuse me of doing. I tried to pluck some certainty out of the confusion:

"But *didn't* you Russell? I thought you said earlier that you *had* made a claim on your insurers."

"No Paul. I made a claim to the company's insurers; the company owned the cars. You see? It was *the company's* insurers, not *mine*....."

Indeed, I did see. Obviously this was not a man whose word was in any circumstances to be trusted. He had made an art form of the weasel word.

So he was a convicted fraudster and the story which the Sun had run on its front page was very substantially, if not entirely true. There would certainly be no retraction from the newspaper now. In the circumstances we didn't even try to get one. The headline had accused Russell King of being a convicted insurance fraudster and that was exactly what he was. His days of having anything to do with the day to day operation of Notts County Football Club, still less being the public face of the Club and escorting Helen Mulcahy to her seat on television, were well and truly over. Just like that. In a heartbeat.

From this point on Notts County embarked on a policy, on our advice, of distancing itself publicly as much as it could from Russell King. The Club made this clear in various pronouncements; including assurances given to the Football League as its Regulator. Behind the scenes I am pretty sure, especially now with the benefit of hindsight, that Russell King was still pulling the strings and those who were in control at Meadow Lane were still regularly consulting him in the months that lay ahead; in fact I am sure that was the case, but publicly at least, he had ceased to have any involvement with its day to day operations.

This was as good as a formal admission that King was not a fit and proper person to be involved in the running of a Football Club (which, indeed, he obviously wasn't). So it could now only be a matter of time before the Takeover Panel expressed their own concerns as to his fitness and propriety to be involved in the takeover of a publicly listed company. Twenty four hours was all it took as it turned out; it must surely be the first time in the history of the City of London that the Takeover Panel has made an intervention on the basis of a front page story in the Sun Newspaper. There was, of course, no answer to that intervention either and we almost immediately backed Russell King away from the SCH deal as well.

To be fair he had probably lost interest in it by that stage.

But Derek Tread hadn't lost interest; the proposed takeover of First London was to take another, unexpected twist but not before Her Majesty's Revenue and Customs had started asking awkward questions about the Football Club.

Penelope

In Homer's Odyssey Penelope lives a broadly unspoken existence on Ithaca for the twenty years odd years it took Odysseus to sail off to Troy, fight with the Trojans, hide in a horse and then make his way back home (I am paraphrasing there; read the book, it is much more highly textured). During those twenty years Penelope successfully fended off the horde of unruly young and old men looking to marry her by telling them that she would decide on the lucky spouse to be only after she had finished weaving a cloak to wear on her wedding day. So she would weave all day and then unpick her work by night which is why the cloak still wasn't finished twenty years later when Odysseus finally returned home. Penelope was canny that way.

And that was pretty much how I dealt with Keith Brentford at First London after Milbank Tweed had been given their marching orders by Derek Tread and Russell King. On balance I would say that my experience over this period suggested that Milbanks were not actually as indispensable to the transaction as I had been led to expect they were, but there again the long telephone calls with Keith Brentford (which I was now being subjected to instead) made me almost long for the old daily briefings with Stuart Harray: working every day with Keith Brentford was *that* bad.

What I would do, just like Penelope did, would be to spend the day working on the Offer Document; making grammatical and stylistic changes for the most part, but also correcting points of substance, such as who owned what and where (still a particularly thorny issue but I was doing my best to get to grips with it as best I could; for the most part

137

Russell King was still holding the line that it would be deeply offensive to his paymaster in Bahrain even to *ask* who owned SCH). Then, just as Penelope had done, Keith Brentford would spend the evening and, so it seemed, most of the night, unpicking all the changes which I had made during the day; then he would weave in various, wholly arbitrary changes of his own. The result was that the Offer Document was worked on almost constantly over this period on a daily basis but it never actually progressed in any way towards anything remotely resembling the finished article.

It was difficult enough trying to understand why Brentford had introduced any one of these thousands of corrections and "improvements"; often he would move a single word three places further on in the sentence for no apparent reason where it would stand out like a sore thumb on a flat foot; or he would change English spellings to American spellings (to be fair he was an American, they are fussy about these things, but this was, after all, an English document for domestic consumption); often he would seem to do both things at the same time, but then he never used tracked changes so it was almost impossible to find out exactly what he had done beyond the obvious awful mangled language that his efforts had left behind in their wake. I was little better I suppose. I didn't really know what I was doing either, but at least I was trying not to murder the English language in the process.

It was because of this, because I was finding it so hard to work out what Keith Brentford did by night (on the document at least, I had no interest in what he did otherwise, the evenings were his to do with what he wanted); it was because of this constant change process that he and I had been compelled to have regular afternoon calls to go over the document and check it was all in shape; which of course it wasn't, far from it, the document was showing the scars of mangling and ever advancing illiteracy every day. It was almost frightening to watch, and the sheer horror of these calls, which would sometimes take up a whole afternoon, made me almost long for the days when my diary was blighted by Stuart Harray. But worse even than that, when Keith Brentford and I were unable to agree on any particular drafting point he would appeal to Derek Tread to break the deadlock; and whenever this happened he would halt the call midstream and try to "patch" Derek Tread in; on a good day Tread would not be around to be patched in but otherwise, when available, he would invariably come down against the inclusion of any legalese and red tape in this Frankenstein's monster of a document; which meant that he would invariably reject out of hand any comments that I might have made (because I was a lawyer).

The Offer Document grew in this way; it grew and grew; swelling to over three hundred pages of closely typed, single spaced garbage; and it was as ugly as hell. I was ashamed to show it to anybody. If this hideous thing were human and related to the Royal family they would have chained it up in their attic.

But Keith Brentford didn't seem to care; on and on we worked on this terrible thing, never getting a day closer to finishing it. In fact every day we got further

140

and further away from finishing it and the process was gradually wearing me down. I took a family holiday in South Africa towards the end of the year and spent more or less every day on the phone with Brentford, reviewing his changes; debating their worth, shouting with Derek Tread, and missing my children on the beach while the document grew uglier still. My holidays were all like that back then. It was while I was on holiday in South Africa that Helen Mulcahy had told me for the first time about the First London Guarantee; about the exciting new signing of Kasper Schmeichel at Notts County and about the beguiling prospect of David Beckham joining the Club. So that cheered me up a little. It wasn't all mind numbingly bad.

But if Keith Brentford and I were showing signs of not caring, that was certainly not the case for the folk over at the City Takeover Panel. They, in sharp contrast, were showing a keen interest in this project; not least because I had by now told them that I would be dealing with them on the drafting process without any input from Milbank Tweed and they were instantly suspicious. They sensed, rightly, that I was not altogether sure of what I was doing and by this stage; of course, the clock had already struck thirteen for them following the disclosures in the *Sun* about Russell King and his Aston Martins. To put it mildly, the Takeover Panel were now excessively wary of the whole project.

I doubted that the Takeover Panel could be made in any way comfortable by sharing with them the latest draft of the Offer Document; that was if anything only likely to frighten them off still further, either that or to ask for three or four hefty men to call round to my office and have me taken off in a straightjacket. So I made a policy decision to take a different course with them; I decided to test just a single aspect of the transaction with the Panel at a time; put to them one critical piece of the jigsaw and invite them to say whether they would be happy with it or not. In that way I hoped to make at least some incremental, piecemeal progress without bringing the whole pack of cards crashing down around my ears in one go.

The Takeover Panel are good in that way; I may on occasions here have given the impression that they are tetchy and sharp toothed, but nothing could be further from the truth. They are very constructive and open minded and staffed with very bright people who can be of immense assistance in smoothing out the inevitable bumps along the way in a transaction. They had, it is true, objected to Russell King being involved in SCH following the *Sun* article; but there again I agreed with them on that one. He was a crook.

Piecemeal and Professor Mendelson

The issue which I chose to review with the Takeover Panel in this way was the robustness or otherwise of the asset agreement entered into between Swiss Commodity Holding and the North Korean Government. The Panel would need to be assured, to put it mildly, that the agreement was watertight because the assets in North Korea which the Agreement was designed to unlock comprised the *sole* asset of any value which was being offered to existing First London shareholders in exchange for their shares. Save for this Swiss Commodity Holding had no other assets whatsoever. So the Panel would be particularly interested in issues such as whether the agreement could be readily enforced to ensure that the North Korean State properly performed its side of the bargain; whether it was sufficiently clear as to the classes of mineral assets which it regulated and how those assets would be got out of the ground (because however extensive it might be, a seam of coal locked irretrievably five miles under the South China Sea is worth nothing); and then there were the difficult Public International Law issues; would the agreement be enforceable at all as a matter of public policy, was it properly executed and was it registered, as it had to be, as a Bilateral Trade Treaty. Things like that.

I felt that if we could nail those points down effectively then it might be possible, for once, to rise above the floundering and document mauling we had been engaged in for the past fortnight and to make some real progress. I was planning to draft a short standalone section dealing with the robustness of the covenants in the asset agreement and I would send it to the Takeover Panel for comment. But more than that, and with more than half an eye to the fact that we had undoubtedly lost a lot of traction with the Panel in the light of the stories that had been run about Russell King in the *Sun*, I thought I should also buttress the drafting with an opinion from a leading QC specialising in Public International Law. That would have the added advantage that I could then bask in the reflected glory of the QC's brilliance.

Of course I also had in mind that if the asset agreement came up to snuff following such a review then it would to a very considerable extent allay the niggling but now increasing suspicion I had that all might not be well with SCH and Russell King; I was, after all, still sitting on a bill from Milbank Tweed for £92,000 which my firm would have to pay and where, for obvious reasons, I wanted every scrap of reassurance I could get as to SCH's standing and its ability to reimburse us for this outlay as and when we came to pay it. If the asset agreement was solid then the likelihood was that SCH was solid too and we could expect, as much as one ever can expect anything in an uncertain world, that we would not end up £92,000 out of pocket; not to mention the not insignificant fact (to me at least) that my firm had still to be paid our own fees for acting on the transaction whatever was or wasn't due to be paid to Milbank Tweed. It would be good to know those fees would be paid too. Testing the asset agreement was a way of checking how solid the ground was that we were all standing on.

I had been sent a copy of the asset agreement by Russell King on the day we were first instructed on the First London transaction. It was not a long document; just three or four pages, and it looked pretty much like the kind of thing that might emerge from negotiations between a Swiss Company and a team of technocrats acting on behalf of the North Korean State; at least it was in English so I could read it and the North Korean's English was a lot better than the English routinely deployed by Keith Brentford. The document also had a large red ideogramic seal on each page which looked as though it could well have emanated from the North Korean

Government; it looked official and the seal itself was broadly unintelligible (just what you would expect from a nation state). But was it the real thing? I remember turning the pages over seemingly endlessly that afternoon; was it the real thing?

I telephoned Russell King to get things going on the new strategy:

"Russell, we're making heavy weather with the Takeover Panel at the moment......"

"Don't tell me you want to get Milbank Tweed back on board. They're useless."

I decided not to rise to that one.

"No, not that Russell; but I do want to do something to achieve a little more traction in our exchanges with the Panel. What I want to do is to have a senior barrister experienced in Public International Law, to look at the asset agreement and produce an opinion on the robustness of its terms; whether they can be enforced, what they all mean in terms of a Bilateral Trade Treaty; and you know Russell, I am also very conscious that we had no involvement in the preparation of the document so I think those are questions that we should look to get answers to regardless of what we need to be telling the Takeover Panel. If this agreement is just a scrap of worthless paper, my view is that you should look to find that out now before we spend any further time and money on the transaction. What do you think?"

I held my breath.

At that time, of course, I never suspected in any concrete way that the agreement was anything other than genuine; there might be questions on what it all meant, but a fabrication? No. Having said that though, the heady mix of having a £92,000 bill sitting on my desk and a convicted insurance fraudster on the other end of the telephone did make me more than usually interested in what Russell King had to say in answer. If this whole thing was all smoke and mirrors, which was my nightmare niggle, then Russell King would presumably not want the terms of the asset agreement tested. So in a way it was better that I should know that now too; whatever he wanted to do, if the whole thing was smoke and mirrors then I would get out now; and so I had determined to drop him and pull out if he refused to take my advice.

But he didn't say no:

"That's a great idea Paul. Did you have any particular barrister in mind?"

He never said *"barrister"*; he said *"member of my learned friends"* but even now my keyboard resiles from reducing some of his more pompous bullshit into reported speech.

I did have a barrister in mind; Maurice Mendelson QC, Master of the Bench of Lincoln's Inn, adviser to a slew of Governments around the world on bilateral investment treaties; counsel to the Bank of England, counsel to the Council of Europe, Inmarsat and the

European Commission; expert witness to the House of Lords select Committee on the Arctic; Chair of International Law at University College London (my own alma mater); sometime Lecturer in Law at Oxford University and Visiting Professor of International Law at the Institut des Hautes Etudes Internationales in Paris; sometime Visiting Professor of International law at the University of New South Wales; Visiting Professor of International Law at the University of Pennsylvania (another alma mater of mine); Visiting Scholar at Harvard School of Law; an Officer De L'Ordre de la Valour awarded by the Republic of Cameroon; a sometime Kennedy Law Scholar and, ladies and gentlemen, the winner of the Association for European Law Prize in 1977.

Yes, that's right, *that* Maurice Mendelson.

"He sounds alright Paul, if you think he's OK; let's go for him."

"Great, I'll get some papers out to him this afternoon Russell. Let me just ask you this as well though; just before I let you go. As I mentioned, my firm wasn't involved in the drafting and preparation of the asset agreement, I think it would be helpful for me and for Mendelson to see something of the background to that as well. Would you be able to let me know which Law Firm was involved in that on behalf of Swiss Commodity Holding; I assume it was a London Law Form because the agreement is in English and subject to English Law; but is that right Russell, who was it? Were you involved at the time?"

"I was Paul, yes."

"So can you let me know who it was?"

"Yup, it was Norton Rose. Do you know them?"

I did know them.

Norton Rose are a very substantial international law firm based on London's South Bank; they would re-emerge in this story shortly in a different role but for the moment it was heartening for me to hear that SCH had used such a substantial and well known law firm on the original transaction; first because they were unlikely to have screwed it up so it was unlikely to cause any major bumps down the road and, secondly, which was at the time almost as important to me, the fact that Norton Rose had prepared the asset agreement on behalf of SCH made it much less likely, at least to my mind, that the whole thing was just a mess of smoke and mirrors; there are many law firms who specialise in the production of mirrors and smoke; but Norton Rose is not one of them.

So I was cheered to hear what Russell King had to say on this front; and the fact that he was so readily giving me the green light to have the agreement reviewed and tested by the great Mendelson was further cause for cheer.

But of course, Russell King wouldn't be Russell King unless there was also a straw of gloom in the wind:

"Great, and could you let me know who the partner was at Norton Rose who dealt with the transaction; I can talk with him or her and get hold of the file, that should help us a lot in getting together a good, solid boiler plated opinion for the Panel. And you of course."

"Ah, well now.........let me see; I'm not sure if I can remember who that was Paul; let me think........."

I gave him a moment, he had been doing so well so far that it seemed peevish to push him.

"........let me think now. Actually, you know what, I think he is on sabbatical. In fact I'm pretty sure, yes, he's on sabbatical in Greece or somewhere for the next six months but leave it with me and I'll see what I can do to get hold of him. What *was* his name now?

He appeared to be trying hard to remember the name; he *appeared* to be....

"Well, shall I call Norton Rose and try and find out for you; can you remember which department there dealt with the transaction?"

"No, don't worry about that Paul. Leave it with me.......I must be getting old; I can't remember the guy's name for the life of me but I'm sure he is on sabbatical at the moment, I got an e-mail from him.........Let me see if I can find the e-mail, that ought to be a start........."

And so he wound on. Old blubber lips, blubbing away like a contestant on *Just a Minute* with the sole intention of stopping me from asking again for clearance to contact Norton Rose directly on SCH's behalf. Because, of course, Norton Rose had not acted in the transaction at all; they had nothing to do with it and direct contact of that kind could bring the whole subterfuge crashing down. So he blubbed on to keep it hanging in the air for as long as possible and eventually I put him out of his blubbery misery and ended the call. But I didn't know these things at the time; at the time I was happy because we could, at last, dig into the core of the transaction and get some verifiable facts and the pursuit of verifiable facts was, at that stage, very high up on my agenda.

Professor Mendelson got his papers later that evening.

The Formula One Team

Within a week, and much to my delight, Professor Mendelson had come up with the goods. Indeed, he had done some admirable digging of his own in the absence of anything even approximating to a file relating to the negotiation and execution of the asset agreement. He had found out, for example, that the agreement had been properly registered with the relevant United Nations trade entities in Geneva so that it was looking good as a bona fide international investment treaty. No smoke and mirrors there. In addition, he had been over the terms of the Agreement with a fine tooth comb and found that it all held together with the rigour that he would expect from an agreement of this sort (I wasn't wholly sure whether that qualification was a good or a bad thing). If anything, he thought the agreement was *too* robust; he described it as "leonine" with its terms being almost uniformly tilted in favour of SCH and against the North Koreans; to the extent that he thought there might be any danger or risk in the document it was this leonine character of the drafting; the danger was that it might generate an undue sense of sympathy in the North Korean's favour should there be any later dispute within the scope of the arbitral provisions in the deed. I called Professor Mendelson up to ask him whether this was a substantial issue or one of impression only; I could live with the prospect of some arbitrator in Zurich feeling sorry for North Korea in five years' time; somebody had to feel sorry for them. Not, however, if the clause didn't work at all. But I was assured by the Professor that the clause was perfectly fine; this was a matter of impression only so I told him it was an interesting issue and then swept it from my mind.

Things were looking good. I had seen the asset agreement and it worked.

Russell King was pleased when I told him; as well he might be, and so were the Takeover Panel when I gave them a sniff of the Mendelson opinion; I had decided by this stage to hold back a full copy of the opinion until we had developed the progress a little further; in legal practice as in life generally, it is usually best to leave your public wanting more and for this purpose the team at the Takeover Panel were my public; them and Russell King.

My next move was to get an equivalent level of clarity on just what all of these North Korean assets were worth. As I have mentioned already, it was all very well to point to the El Dorado of gold and silver and uranium and shale slips of other minerals which the agreement covered, but all of that wealth was still deep in the North Korean countryside, in some instances indeed under the South China Sea, and just what was it worth while it was all still in the ground? As best I knew nobody was actively looking at actual exploitation of the mineral reserves; still less transporting assets to markets where they could be

157

sold for hard cash; primarily meaning, of course, the Chinese markets which had at that time a virtually insatiable appetite for minerals from coal to bronze (all of which we had and Uranium too, dare we but talk about it). Nobody was talking about exploiting the reserves at that level yet, for the very good reason that exploitation on that scale would cost millions. The plan, rather, was to use the value inherent in the asset agreement to carry out an initial fundraising (there was talk of an initial public offer in SCH on the Hong Kong Market) as a prelude to exploitation.

But, in the meantime I still needed to include a valuation for all of these buried assets in the Offer Document; SCH was offering its assets, though its shares, in exchange for shares in First London so we obviously needed to know what the assets were worth.

I was introduced, for this purpose, to Stephen White (not his real name); Stephen was an accountant and an expert in preparing valuations of this kind for the purpose of public offering certifications. I was still feeling the wind beneath my wings through the blessings afforded by the Mendelson opinion so finding Stephen in such short order afterwards was a double cause for celebration. For the first time in the transaction, and as it happens also for the last time, I was working in a brief window of expectancy where it felt as though it might just be possible to pull this off.

Such moments tended to coincide with those brief fleeting periods when I had not spoken with Russell King for a day or so; and there was, of course, no particular surprise about that either then or now; King was a malign influence capable of polluting everything that he touched.

Stephen and I had worked for a couple of days in setting the framework for his opinion within the scope of the draft Offer Document which I was now reasonably hopeful of pulling back into shape (I had not spoken with Keith Brentford for a week or so either by this stage, not since halting the general drafting process and going off to Professor

Mendelson; so much was a cause for celebration too).
Through the process of working with Stephen we
found the component parts of the valuation gradually
falling into place. As I say, for the first (and last) time
I thought the whole thing might just be possible.

That was all to change when I was asked by Stephen
to mediate the completion of his firm's client care
letter on behalf of SCH; he asked me, not
unreasonably, to find out from Russell King who the
owners of SCH were:

> "Tell him to fuck off; that's got nothing to do with
> him."

> "Well, Russell, it does have a lot to do with him
> actually; he can't sign off his retainer with SCH
> unless he knows who the ownership interests are,
> and if he can't do that he won't produce the
> valuation on the North Korean assets. It just won't
> happen. So it does have a lot to do with him and
> with us; if he doesn't produce the valuation we
> won't have a transaction to do. I don't want to be

difficult but that's the position. We need him Russell. You need to tell me who is behind this company. I want to know too, it's not just for the valuation."

In a sense I was almost pleading with him to tell me; it seemed to be such a waste to let all the work we had done over the past month go to waste because he wanted to be coy about who in Bahrain actually owned SCH. Kevin Leech had in any event already told me that it was owned by members of the Bahraini Royal Family for whom Russell King was acting as a front man. Why should it be so difficult to be explicit with me if he had already given the details to Kevin Leech?

"Why is this so difficult Russell? I just don't understand that, if you can share some of the reasons with me we can try to work them through but we need this valuation report, as I say; and we won't get it without client verification."

"Get another valuer then."

I had seen that one coming; it would then be Milbank Tweed all over again, but this time with a twist:

"But that will solve nothing Russell; any new valuer will want the same information; we are dealing with a highly regulated market here. I need you to help us or we won't get anywhere."

It was becoming a very serious conversation; Russell King was cracking none of his usual, fatuous witticisms.

"Well, OK, I can see that Paul; can you have Stephen come and see Nathan and me at the Dorchester tomorrow morning and we'll see if we can work something out; it is really not the sort of thing that either of us will want to put on paper or in an e-mail. I can see what you're saying though; have him come over to the Dorchester tomorrow morning and we'll sort something out. I promise."

In all honesty it did sound as though he understood what I was saying; and, seemingly for the first time, what Stephen had also been telling him. It was a pivotal moment; quite literally a pivotal moment. It was the end of my period of expectancy and the beginning of a series of increasingly bizarre incidents that would see the whole adventure fall to pieces within a matter of two months.

When I arrived with Stephen at the Dorchester the next day I was at the very least expecting Russell King and Nathan Willett to provide Stephen, at least orally, with an outline of the shareholding interests in SCH. On any construction of our closing comments at the telephone the previous day, Russell King had promised at least that much. So, it was to say the least, a surprise that we should then sit down together only to be told the same old puffery about the scale and significance of the SCH interests in North Korea; it seemed that whenever they were cornered, as they obviously felt themselves to be now, Russell King and Nathan Willett would respond by throwing pixie dust in the air in the shape of billion dollar return figures and world domination of the minerals market (the newspapers had even christened SCH, with obvious justification, "the biggest minerals company you've never heard of"); and here they were the two of them throwing pixie dust in our eyes yet again as a substitute for hard facts. It was exasperating but it was also, this morning at least, bewildering because I listened to Stephen lap up every last detail (this was his first direct exposure to King and Willett); he was nodding and purring on cue and rapidly agreeing that in the circumstances of this transaction, there was really no need to produce a detailed valuation at all. It would be enough to certify that the value of the asset reserves in North Korea "massively" exceeded the market value of the transaction to acquire First London's shares. That was totally against everything that Stephen and I had set out by way of the framework document for the valuation. All of it went out the window in the face of King and Willett's special kind of magic.

More than that, I was simply aghast to hear right at the cusp of the meeting closing that Russell King was assuring Stephen that there was no need for him to ask any questions *at all* about the SCH ownership interests:

"You see Stephen……..

King was panting like a man climbing a steep hill through the very effort of speaking and breathing at the same time; he rolled back in his chair:

"…………I am the agent for various interests of the Bahraini Royal family. They are as you might imagine very secretive and not at all anxious to have the Royal Family's private affairs splattered across the media; and there is one thing we know for sure, which is when this Offer Document or whatever it is, when this Offer Document is filed for public inspection, the press will be all over it and I cannot allow that to happen; I have an obligation to protect the Royal Family's interest in their privacy. I do hope you understand that Stephen."

Willett was nodding sagely as all this came out; King was puffing like billy o.

"Of course Russell, and thank you both for seeing me this morning; that's fine; of course it is. We don't need to press any further; I will go ahead and put together the valuation on the basis of what we have already. I didn't mean to trouble you. As I say it's good of you to take the time to see me this morning and to explain everything."

As I say, Pixie Dust.

It seemed we were never going to find out who was behind SCH and, indeed, we never did.

After Stephen had left I took my seat again and Willett leant into me in conspiratorial fashion. His thick sausage fingers toying with the piece of paper in front of him, he scooped up a biro and wrote very deliberately, speaking as he wrote like a dim child learning his alphabet: Kew – Ay – Dee – Bah – Ay - Kay.

"You see what that spells?"

He was pointing with his middle sausage finger to the acronym on the page, written by him in heavy capitals; and he was looking at me with the nascent pride of a syphilitic who has just discovered penicillin.

I did see:

"I do".

"Qadbak".

"Yes".

He leant back in his seat.

"You know what that stands for?"

"No."

"It stands for....Qatar, Abu Dhabi, Bahrain and Kuwait".

I felt in my heart that it was inappropriate to include the *"and"* as one of the *A*'s; that looked a bit like cheating acronym-wise, but at least it rendered the whole thing euphonious. But I didn't tell him that. He was my client.

"Really; I see. Obviously I've seen the name before but I didn't know what it stood for.....No. I didn't know that."

He was now looking even more smug than usual.

"Yes, this is one of the biggest Sovereign Wealth Funds in the world. I just wanted to let you know who was behind the Project".

I shrugged with my eyes to express a sense of awe as best I could.

"Don't tell Uncle Derek this because he'll be cross with us but we have another Project we're looking at. We've been really pleased with the work you've been doing for the football club.......So we want you to act for Qadbak in its purchase of Sauber. The deal is signed up in principle but we want you to do the legal work and get everything finished off; preferably over the course of the next few days. Do you think you might be able to do that? Would that be OK?"

I tried to upgrade the impression of awe but in actual fact I didn't know what on earth Sauber was so it was difficult to express adequately the sense of veneration that Willett so obviously felt it deserved.

"You're probably asking yourself why we're going to buy Sauber; what it has to do with SCH........."

That was a difficult one to express a view on as well given I had no idea who or what Sauber was. So instead I tilted my head to one side slightly which is often mistaken as a sign of thinking profoundly on an issue.

Willett shuffled from side to side to work up the momentum he needed to emerge from the depths of the armchair into which his bulk had sunk; once free he leaned into me again and hushed his secret:

"*Steel*...............BMW are a great market for steel under the DPRK contract".

Well, I could certainly see that so now I was able to venture a tentative "*oh yes*". Had I known then what I found out later when I got back to the office, I might also have said that BMW's decision to divest itself of its holding in the Sauber Formula 1 Racing Team was a unique opportunity for a Sovereign Wealth Fund with QADBAK's ambitions; or some such bullshit. But not knowing that then, I merely said:

"*Oh yes*".

"Yes indeed. I'll give you the name of the lawyer at Norton Rose who is acting for BMW; if you can give him a call this afternoon, I think he's keen to get into some of the detail with a view to putting the documentation together over the weekend".

Willett went on to tell me that the deal to buy the BMW Sauber Team had to be completed by 11.00am on the following Monday (I was talking with him on the Friday afternoon); otherwise the whole thing was dead in the water. On Monday the Governing body of Formula One, ruled over by the diminutive Bernie Ecclestone (more of him in a moment too) would allocate grid places and without an owner there would be no place on the grid for Sauber; and without a place on the grid the Team would have as much commercial value as a pair of sandals. This kind of ridiculous, arbitrary time pressure is, as I understand it, commonplace in the commercial law world. For my own part I was used to running litigation that took decades to finish so the time critical nature of the task ahead was something relatively new to me.

Not so critical though to prevent me stopping off between the Dorchester and the City to have a glass of wine and a cigar. And as I sipped and puffed away I thought to myself that this was all very odd and unusual; North Korean Gold and Formula One Racing Teams and Football Teams and Sovereign Wealth Funds. It was certainly out of the usual for me to be dealing with all these things in the same week. I remember thinking, as I finished my drink, that this would either be a stepping stone to greater things or a complete disaster.

And we needed Milbank Tweed again, the time pressures were too great for us to look after the deal on our own. So, it was back to Stuart Harray. Their sacking was reversed. To be fair to them, they took it all in exceptionally good heart and without any sense of suppressed rancour. They seemed even to be excited about the new project.

Both they and we (Milbanks and us) drew some comfort from the Sauber transaction; it would at least address the question that had been gnawing silently at each of us for the past month. Were these people actually for real? The new transaction had the virtue of already being some way down the track; indeed we were being introduced to it at the very end of the track; as we had been told earlier that day, our brief was to complete by first thing on the Monday morning when F1 were to allocate the remaining grid places. And BMW were the counterparty; they were certainly real enough.

I had also spoken that afternoon with Meyrick Cox who was then a director of the Investment Bank, Rothschilds. Rothschilds were advising Qadbak on the deal and the fact they were involved was also a source of considerable comfort to me; it meant that they would have carried out client due diligence on Qadbak themselves so we could be reasonably sure that Qadbak was substantial (the standing of all of the entities that were being bandied about was up until that point still a concern to me). The eminent not to say historic House of Rothschild's wouldn't be acting on a deal for a fly by night or made up company. This was the Bank that had advanced the funds to the

British Government to fight the battle of Waterloo and had funded the construction of the Suez Canal; Rothschild's very name was a byword for propriety all across Europe. Beyond that, however, Meyrick had also gone even further on this deal by vouching publicly for Qadbak's standing; unusually so for an investment banker. For example, he had made a public comment to the press that Qadbak was a *"wholly reputable organisation"*. That was to come back to haunt him later; Rothschilds were subsequently to sack Meyrick when the true nature of Qadbak came to light; but for the moment, that was all down the road and we were all heartened by his public pronouncements on the matter. Quite why he chose to make them at all is, of course, another matter. I still don't understand why he did.

Meyrick Cox was very positive about the whole deal. He stressed the very tight time frame we would all be working to but more in the nature of a challenge than a problem; he arranged for us to have access to the due diligence room and we set ourselves ready to get things moving.

A combined team of City Law and Milbank Tweed lawyers were dispatched to meet with BMW's lawyers (Norton Rose) on London's South Bank. Over the course of the afternoon they thrashed out the outline terms of the deal (known as heads of agreement) and by close of business had started working through the thousands of documents in the due diligence room.

Now, it will be remembered that as part of the process of investigating the ambiguities of the asset agreement which SCH had entered into with the North Koreans, Russell King had told me that the agreement had been drafted by Norton Rose on behalf of SCH; and, indeed, that Russell King had acted as middleman between SCH and Norton Rose for the purpose of putting this documentation together. So it was fair to assume on that basis that Norton Rose would know who Russell King and SCH were. In fact, as we now know, they could not have known about either of them for the simple reason that Russell King was lying.

Norton Rose had not been involved in the North Korean transaction at all; but they pretended that they had been to avoid having to own up to the fact that they knew nothing about it at all. Looking back on things with the benefit of hindsight I still find that staggering and it tells us a lot about the mind-set of the average solicitor in the City of London.

After all, one of the key obligations assumed by Norton Rose in acting on this transaction was to verify that Qadbak actually existed and that it had the corporate standing and powers to enter into a valid transaction to purchase the Sauber Team from BMW. If that was not the case then all of the promises made to BMW by SCH in the documentation (and there were many of them) would be utterly worthless because there would be no entity to enforce them against or, worse, the corporate purchaser did exist but its promises wouldn't be binding because of a prior irregularity; it was a potential legal quagmire to say nothing of the reputational damage to BMW should it be found to have entered into a transaction to sell its prized Formula One Team to a company that didn't exist. In the light of the seriousness of those issues Norton Rose quite properly raised the issue of Qadbak's standing at a very early stage in the transaction.

I answered by telling them that they should know all about Qadbak:

"You acted for them"

"Did we?"

"Oh yes; you may have the client as Russell King but he was acting on behalf of Qadbak. He was the company's agent."

They asked me which lawyer at Norton Rose had acted on the deal but of course Russell King had been unable to tell me when I asked him the same question a week or so earlier; so I couldn't tell them either:

"I don't know; but presumably your client records can be searched by reference to the client's name rather than the name of the partner who was responsible for the client at the time."

And of course they could be. There was no answer to that. Norton Rose said they would check and get back to me if they still required evidence of Qadbak's good standing. That was simply impossible to do because they hadn't acted for them at all, Russell King was lying in saying they had; and, as the astute reader will already have noticed, I had the wrong company in any event. If they had acted on the transaction at all, which they hadn't, they would have acted for SCH in its dealings with North Korea; not with Qadbak. SCH had nothing to do with the Sauber transaction.

Despite all of that I received confirmation the next day that, yes, the records had been checked; and they had found the evidence they required. Qadbak had been their client.

Norton Rose is a law firm with a solid international standing; it is one of the largest and best established law firms in the world. Yet on this crucial issue, and acting as they were on behalf of one of the largest and best established motor manufacturers in the world, they were prepared to confirm that they had acted previously on behalf of Qadbak (their records simply could not have borne that out because such records didn't exist). When BMW were later to claim that they had effectively been duped on the transaction through being beguiled as to the true identity of Qadbak and the people behind it (or more accurately the people who weren't behind it) Norton Rose could have avoided the issue altogether by carrying out their own verification properly.

It is even more staggering to reflect on that bearing in mind that Rothschilds had made statements to much the same effect, and with just as little substance to back them up (that is, none at all) by way of the comments made to the press at the time by their managing director Meryick Cox. Poor old Merrick was sacked for saying what he did.

But that, I suppose, is the way these things go. It was at least imprudent of Milbank Tweed and indeed my own Firm to look to each of these blue blooded institutions to give us comfort on Qadbak's standing but that, for better or worse, was undoubtedly what both of us did. Neither of us should have been so naïve.

We convened again the next day, Saturday morning, to receive a briefing from Rothschilds and Russell King. At this stage the lawyers from Milbank Tweed were picking up mostly only headline documents from the data room; nothing of any particular significance. But various issues were tabled for review and analysis.

For example, we were told that Sauber's number one driver, Robert Kubica, had resigned from the team in the light of BMW's announcement that it was pulling out of Formula One racing. It seemed to me that without a driver it would be difficult to get the cars to go around the track; a view which was shared by others on the team. Their number two driver was still in place but his loyalty was likely to be tested if the new owner wasn't in charge by Monday morning.

Then we were told that that Formula One Racing, the governing body for the sport run by the enigmatic Bernie Ecclestone, had *already* made a provisional decision to hand the last remaining grid space to a newly re-formed Lotus Racing Team; and if he did that, without a place on the Grid, the Sauber Team would be worth zip all. Again, that prospect, or threat as I am sure Ecclestone intended it to be taken, was adding to the pressure. It was certainly a much more profound issue than the potential loss of the team's number one driver.

During my career as a lawyer I had, as I have already mentioned, mostly worked on litigation and disputes where the timeframe is measured in years and sometimes decades; so although an intensive weekend of work was nothing new to me, the Looking Glass world of the corporate lawyers pretty much was. They exuded the appearance of an appetite for remorseless, results driven working; but in fact manifested a surprising tendency to take their eye off the ball. I was surprised to receive a report from the Milbank team in the early hours of Monday morning (when, I still think sensibly, I was already substantially through a bottle of Chablis) where someone had thought it worthwhile spending two hours to create a cover design of a chequered finishing flag and a copy of the client's logo (I certainly didn't that was time any better spent than on the Chablis).

Time rolled on though and without any sleep worthy of the name, we found ourselves facing the harsh light of Monday morning (signalled, as usual, by the sound of the office cleaner firing up her vacuum).

The final deal had been signed off subject to a series of conditions, most important of which was that it would remain conditional and Qadbak would not be obliged to pay over any part of the purchase price if Formula One failed to give the Sauber Team a place on the starting Grid; and that, as I have said, meant reversing the provisional assigned to Team Lotus which had been made the previous week. We had worked all through the weekend to sign up the papers by Monday morning only on the basis of a vague assurance from Bernie Ecclestone that, as long as Qadbak was in place by then as owner of the Sauber team, he would reverse his provisional decision and award the place on the Grid to us. It had been suggested, equally vaguely, at various points over the weekend that Ecclestone would give us until 11.00am London time on Monday morning to finalise the deal (if only on a conditional basis) after which point he would go unconditionally with Lotus. Most of us took that to be an assurance of some sort that Qadbak would have up until 11.00am that day to complete its own deal.

Nothing could have been further from the truth. Shortly before 10.00am on the day of completion, and with the ink on the agreement with BMW and Qadbak barely dry, we learned that there had been a late filing in the data room; it was an agreement definitively vesting the last remaining space on the Grid to Team Lotus. We had worked all through the weekend for nothing. I was concerned that this agreement with Lotus had been filed so very close to the time of physical completion of the agreement with BMW. It was almost as though it had been intended to undermine the conditional provision in the purchase agreement that the deal need not be finalised if the Grid space had already been allocated to someone else; might it be said that the condition was in that light ineffective so that Qadbak would have to pay over the full purchase price and get nothing in return?

Plainly the Alice in Wonderland character of Formula One Racing had more than a little in common with the world of SCH, North Korean Gold and Notts County taking over the Universe. Nothing was what it seemed to be. We had worked for four days flat to complete an agreement that obliged our client to pay nothing, to get nothing and to give nothing back.

Bernie Ecclestone

A week had passed since that completion and I was milling, as one man might, around the fountain in the middle of Sloane Square; checking at one minute intervals to see whether there were any incoming e-mails on my phone. I saw that there were three; all within the space of the last minute and all from the same man; if he might be called a man. Russell King was obviously up and active in Bahrain:

"*Make it clear to Bernie that without Sauber he will have sponsorship isues*".

"Issues" with one "*s*". Literacy was never Russell King's strongpoint.

"*We have Bernie on the ropes on this*".

"*We want vintage Paul on this*".

Sure you do.

I wasn't exactly inspired with confidence.

Since we had finalised the deal to buy the Sauber Team from BMW I had taken part with Russell King in an increasingly strained series of calls with BMW's lawyers; they were asking when we would close and, not unimportantly (for them at least), when Qadbak would pay over the hundred and thirty million pounds it had agreed to pay them. For his part, no doubt feeling the want of a hundred and thirty million pounds, King was making great play of the fact that Sauber had not been given the final place on the Grid (that had gone to Lotus); until that point was sorted out Qadbak felt able to decline to pay over the money that he didn't have. It was a rock and a hard place and the dialogue was getting nowhere.

So BMW were now calling Russell King's bluff and, as corporate lawyers might put it, were facilitating the clearing up of the issue. I was on my way to see Bernie Ecclestone at his Knightsbridge Offices to get some clarity on the Grid Place. It would, indeed, call for "*Vintage Paul*"; but it would also bring up head on a whole load of issues which had more than one "*s*".

I was pretty clear in my own mind that King's confidence and sense of bravura were misplaced.

BMWs team were waiting for me at a hotel around the corner in Sloane Street; there they were, clustered together over coffee. Their lawyer was the obvious leader of the three; she was a charming young woman, thin skinned of average height with short dark hair; almost alone amongst our little group, I suspected, she still believed that there was the remotest chance of this deal coming to anything. She radiated a touching and innocent willingness to believe almost anything. The two hardnosed money men that she had in tow with her were, on the other hand, very much horses of a different colour; they were obviously not so worldly unwise as she was. Indeed. from the very moment of my arrival they were glowering at me; seeming to take even my being at their table, even more my appropriation of some of their coffee and cookies, as an insult matched only by the Versailles Peace Treaty; I half thought the two of them might have been sent over by BMW's higher orders to give me a duffing up for wasting their time. I felt half constrained to confess in mitigation that I was pretty sure Russell King was spinning them along and that at heart he was a modern day Walter Mitty with an appetite for the occasional fraud; might I then be spared?

Their lawyer poured me a strong coffee, I decided on balance to refuse a cookie, as she told me what lay in store for us later:

"I have arranged for us to meet Peter afterwards at the Hilton Hotel in Park Lane. If we cannot sort this out with Bernie, he will certainly want to talk to you to.........see what we can do to get this deal completed".

Peter: that was Peter Sauber; the founder and spiritual force behind the Sauber Formula One Racing Team. Peter Sauber had already met on at least one occasion with Russell King as part of the negotiations leading up to the deal and King had reported back to me that he (Sauber) was a "gentleman". So I could see immediately what BMW were doing by arranging a meeting with him today, and then only if the talks with Ecclestone failed to break the deadlock. They wanted to make clear to me that if the deal didn't come together then we would be breaking Peter Sauber's old heart and I would be required to look him in his old tear filled eyes and tell him why we were doing it.

Talk about killing Bambi.

But at least there was still a chance of persuading Bernie Ecclestone to change his mind. Good old, soft hearted Bernie. He wouldn't force me to break Peter Sauber's heart.

"Bernie, obviously, will be very tough to move on this. He likes to play games. I've been in this situation before and he's really only interested in one thing, wining out for Bernie. So we have to stay pretty focussed".

The briefing from Fraulein BMW 2009 was not filling me with confidence. It was, if anything, draining away my will to live.

I nodded and smiled at her as I tried to drink down my super-heated coffee without melting the roof of my mouth. Even if I could speak through the pain of the coffee, which was frankly doubtful, I couldn't really think of anything to say or do beyond smiling and nodding. It was a one sided conversation.

"Bernie has his office just around the corner in Knightsbridge. I've been there before. We will have………."

She tugged up her tailored sleeve and checked her tiny watch

"……….right we have ten minutes before we have to leave. I've arranged a car which will be outside now, so let's really focus on what we need to do here. I am pretty sure Bernie will let us have the grid place but he will play hard ball before he lets us have it; so keep in focus. The points we really need to stress to him are the standing of the Qadbak company and its position as a natural successor to BMW on this.........."

Ah, yes; the standing of the Qadbak Company. Corporate Titan that it was; I hoped Ecclestone had not read or noticed the reports in the British Press that Qadbak was being run from a shepherd's hut in the border region of Pakistan by a shepherd who had never heard of the company. The Football League might be prepared to buy into that but I doubted whether Bernie Ecclestone would (so the less he knew about it the better). That was obviously the role I was being squared up to play; I was to say as little as I could about Qadbak in as many words as possible.

"You will have to cover that Paul".

She gave me a telling stare and a meaningful pause.

I nodded and smiled back through the pain of the coffee; not quite failing to notice that her two colleagues were still signalling menace in their every fibre.

They wouldn't beat me up in broad daylight would they; surely not in Kensington Gore?

What would they do if I made a run for it?

She was nodding and making very obvious eye contact with me while I was pondering that thorny issue:

"Just give him the details of Qadbak's financial background; as much as you can to give Bernie the assurance he needs that this thing won't just unravel as soon as BMW leave. You will want to play this your own way Paul, but for my part, speaking only for myself, I would say that you can't really give him too much detail on this issue, you know. The more the better; as much as you can. This is, to me, is the real tilting point of the deal; we will do all we can from BMW's side to persuade him of the good standing of your client but you need to really pack the table with data to leave him in no doubt as to just how good a company Qadbak is. Make it a no brainer for him".

What could I do? I agreed with her tactics, the problem was the total absence of table packing data.

I smiled back and nodded.

She was checking her watch again; a brittle little tug of the sleeve.

"Right.......we have to go."

She made a short, slurping performance of finishing off her coffee and stood to go; tugging up her briefcase as she did so.

It was an example we were plainly required to follow but none of us did so with any sense of enthusiasm.

We picked up our things and followed her like three schoolboys being summoned for prayers.

As we shambled towards the lobby, Fraulein BMW getting further ahead of us by the moment, one of the two silent partners caught my arm:

"You know, Bernie is an odd fellow. I heard once that he was in a car park and there was only one space left; he drove like a crazy guy to make sure he was the one that got it. Reversing and stalling round the cars to make sure that he got that one last remaining place. And you know what; when he finally had it, he just waited in his car for the other driver to pull alongside him, behind him; and when he saw him in his rear-view mirror he smiled very obviously back at him, in the mirror, waved and then pulled back to let the other fellow take the place."

He was staring down at me too now, with something of the intensity of his leader, as we ambled along.

"And you know, that's the kind of guy Bernie is. You need to know that. You need to know that so that you know how to deal with him".

I didn't have the slightest clue what he was talking about or what any of that meant.

The car was waiting for us at the front of the hotel. As I suppose was only to be expected, loyalty to the company meant it was a BMW. But it wasn't a sleek limousine type BMW which, if I had been thinking about it, I might have expected (in fact I wasn't thinking at all, I was expecting a black London Taxi); it was a BMW alright but it was a Mini; and there were five of us including the driver (who was, of course, wearing full chauffeur livery, including peaked cap). There was a general pause as we contemplated the crush; and I thought I doubt I was alone in thinking it, that the choice of car marked an atypical falling off in her otherwise manifest talent; I'm pretty sure the chauffeur was thinking that. For a start the other two were enormous physical specimens. Where was I going to sit?

We all five looked down on the Mini which had grown smaller with being looking at.

"It's only round the corner; I think I'll walk if that's OK with you."

I thought that was quite a sensible suggestion given we were only four or five hundred yards from Ecclestone's Office. But no:

"We can't do that. Bernie will think we aren't serious if we don't arrive together."

All this *Bernie* this and *Bernie* that was starting to irritate me; it wasn't as though they were his bosom chums. If anything they gave every appearance of being terrified of the man.

But the Mini wasn't getting any bigger by being looked at.

They used to run competitions to find out how many (usually students) could fit into a Mini; if the students were as large and knotted with muscle and fat as these two, then the answer, far from fifty three, would be four (two in the back and two in the front); so where was I going to sit?

In some discomfort as it turned out, and on the back seat, between the two of them.

As the Mini pulled away, straining and almost visibly buckling under the weight of its unusual load, we all three in the back were blinded by our briefcases; with no leg, foot or any other room below clavicle level, we all three were reduced to holding our bags inches in front of our faces; arms locked in vertical rictus to avoid intruding on each other's, for want of a better phrase although the phrase itself was risible in the circumstances, "personal space".

"So, what we need to do is for you, Paul…."

She twisted round as best she could to look at me from the front seat:

"……is for you, Paul, to give as much detail about Qadbak as you can to Bernie…….."

It was Bernie again.

"…..as much as you can; all the financial data you have available so that Bernie can be comfortable in knowing that BMW can cease to have anything to do with the team……..That things will go on smoothly with Qadbak in charge after……..You see?"

She was attempting to smile but the car wasn't big enough.

"Yes. I see."

Where was Meyrick Cox when you needed him? Sacked, that's where he was.

She eased herself back into a forward posture. And the car struggled on.

I was surprised that Ecclestone's Office (Bernie to the rest of us) looked so much like his house; but as I was later to find out, his office was on the ground floor of his house so it all made sense really. The house was an enormous five story Edwardian Building on Kensington Gate; the office was surprisingly small. Like the car we had just been shoehorned out of; well maybe not quite *that* small. I ought to have been surprised too by the platinum blond supermodel who was posing as a Receptionist as we went in; and she had a clone in the other platinum blonde supermodel whose job was to make the tea and show visitors through to the meeting room. But somehow I wasn't surprised about that. *That* was what I had expected.

To avoid a repeat briefing from the Fraulein, I asked to sit in a caucus room on my own ostensibly so as to collect my thoughts until Bernie was ready for us. Happily (for me), she thought that was a good idea too. After the Mini, the feeling of space in that little room was a blessed relief. Despite the smallness of the room someone had thought it was a good idea to screw half of the wing of a formula one car (at least that's what I thought it was) to the wall and pass it off as sculpture; complete with a little brass finger beneath with the "artist's" name and date. I didn't care; I was glad, at last, to have some elbow room and I was certainly not planning on reading through or even thinking about any of the papers I had brought with me. Such as they were, they didn't say a lot anyway.

So I just sat and waited for something to happen.

It took a long time to happen; two hours at least.

Of course I knew all about what one of my client's had once sneeringly described as "*small man syndrome*"; the mind-set of power that assigns visitors to a smaller chair, lower down and literally beneath contempt; and of course I knew that Bernie was a little man (with a penchant for very tall, thin women apparently, such as the two who were buzzing around at the moment outside). So, reflecting as I did on the dynamics of power while I wiled away the idle time, it came as no surprise to me that Bernie had obviously decided to keep us waiting. There were regular offers of coffee and cookies from the two super models so it wasn't as though we weren't being looked after while we waited; and in all honesty I was glad to have a little rest. On the other hand, I was pretty sure the Frauline and her friends were getting edgy next door and that, no doubt, was exactly what Bernie intended.

I didn't care.

When the door opened again later and didn't disclose a supermodel head at six feet two level, I naturally looked down to handle height and there was Bernie; a familiar face from television but someone who I had not at that time (or any time since) met; but, as with so many of the television famous, it *felt* as though I knew him and I greeted him as though he was one of my oldest and smallest friends. I think that may have beguiled him into thinking that he either did or should have known *me*:

"Sorry to keep you waiting. I've asked Dan to take the meeting because I'm rushing around. Hope that's OK……"

"That's fine by me Bernie."

He was grinning up at me from the height of the door handle, which he was holding with both hands as though it were an emergency exit and swinging to and fro on it like a child.

There was a pause because he obviously didn't know who I was and I wasn't about to help him. Not knowing my name was proving a barrier to casual chit chat. So he swung a little more on the door and tried to look as though he was thinking what to say next; who knows maybe he *was* thinking what to say next.

Then he left. He left without saying another word. It was all very odd.

The meeting with Dan was a disaster. It transpired that the decision to give the final grid place to Lotus was pretty much irrevocable; and despite deploying the little charm they had between them as best they could, the BMW delegation were making heavy weather of opening up a "space for review"; in short, the team Sauber was worth so much scrap metal and rubber. It would not be racing in the coming season or, as best I could see, any other season for that matter. Dan was very nice about it all; he was sorry and all that, but no matter how we pleaded the decision had been made and it was all out of his hands. He would love to look at things again but the slot on the grid had already been given out; to Lotus (as we knew), but it was good of us all to come in and see him (apparently); and he thought it was really great to see us; so at least the morning hadn't been a complete waste of time.

Looking on the bright side, at least I hadn't been called on to say anything about Qadbak's financial standing; the Fraulein had on several occasions tipped me what would be known as "the wink" to get me to say something. I just thought it was all really a bit of a waste of time to delude Dan, as I knew I must if I tried to; so I just thought it best not to bother. I let her wink fall on deaf ears.

Also looking on the bright side, the Mini had gone when we made it outside. Re-assigned I hoped to a team of BMW midgets who would find it more comfortable than us. We were free to take a taxi and the relief was palpable. You could have cut it with a knife.

"So now we have to go and see Peter Sauber............."

I had forgotten him.

The familiar hand shot the familiar sleeve to check her watch; then she scuffled around in her handbag to pull out a phone and check on whereabouts and timing. As to whereabouts; Peter Sauber was killing time in the burger bar at the Hilton and, yes, that would be an excellent place to meet; good for me too:

I thought there was less chance of being duffed up in a burger bar and there was no chance of getting duffed up in the cab; so I was safe for an hour or so and home free if I could sneak out of the Hilton unnoticed. And as for timing:

"Yes Peter, we are on our way in the taxi now..............Yes, he's here with me; he is aware of the consequences.................Not that good but I'll tell you all about it when we get there..............No. We saw Dan............No. I don't know his second name........."

She seemed to edge in closer then to her phone, pulling it tighter and almost whispering; but I heard her all the same:

"Not good. He will tell you when we get there.........."

"*He*", that was *me*; I could almost hear the grating sound of the buck being pushed towards me. She finished her call. All three of them were now beyond the threshold of social banter, to the extent, that is, we had ever been close to it in the first place. We tumbled towards the Hilton in a frosty silence.

I have seldom met anyone with the inherent dignity and worth of Peter Sauber. He was a genuinely splendid man. Unlike the rest of us, he had done an honest day's work in his life and his noticeably large and sensitive hands, which I was fascinated by as we took our seats beside him, were splayed on the Formica topped table in front of him as though he was trying to read his own fortune in the minutiae of his fingernails. We had come from a luxury hotel that morning to meet this man in a burger bar. Somehow it was appropriate to his earthiness. His long suit wasn't bullshit; he cut straight to the chase:

"So, it didn't go so well then..........."

"No. We didn't get to see Bernie after all. Do you know Dan Proctor?"

Peter Sauber paused and seemed to scour a lifetime of memories and faces:

"No."

It was hardly a surprise. I imagine the world of Formula One Racing Teams was a lot different now to that which Peter Sauber had grown up with; in his days, for one, there was a risk of coming into contact with motor oil. Now it was a lot more like the World the Frauline, me and the bankers lived in every day; full of faceless accountants who all looked one the same as the other, wearing the same smiles and guilt.

"A decision has already been made to assign the last grid place to Lotus, Peter; but Dan told us that they were open to reviewing that at some point in the future. Just not for the moment."

I couldn't actually remember Dan saying that. But no doubt she was trying to soften the blow and who was I to disagree; as the conversation unwound Peter Sauber seemed to be very close to tears.

207

"So, what we need to look at now is how we go forward with the deal. I know you've been speaking with Russell King Peter and it would be good to know when we can expect the funds to be made available. Maybe Paul could give us the up to date position on that?"

I was about to suggest that we order some burgers, but Peter Sauber cut in before I could say anything:

"I have had a lot of promises from Russell King. He is always going to send funds, or make the funds available......But he never does. I am tired of him telling me that. He is not an honest man......I want to get the funds now or the deal is off. I am not prepared to wait and receive more of these false promises every day..........."

At that point he seemed to run out of emotional steam; he had been flapping his enormous hands emphatically on the table in front of him as he made each point and we were each more or less mesmerised by the performance. So when he came to a halt, an uncomfortable silence took hold.

Russell King is not an honest man.

He might be onto something there.

As they were all looking to me to say something, I thought I better had:

"Well……. Mr Sauber……..I can understand why you say that……..Obviously I can…….We none of us want to be in the position we're in but Russell has been waiting for clarification from F1 and obviously the news this morning isn't good……….I don't know what he will want to do, but without a Grid Place, I'm not sure there are any certainties on this at the moment".

"I just want him to do what he has said he will do; he has signed an agreement to buy……….I just want him to deliver on that and not bullshit us………."

We all do Mr Sauber. We all do.

But of course I couldn't say *that*. I fell instead into mouthing a few platitudes so as to try to finish off the meeting as quickly as possible:

"Well, let me talk with him and I'll see what we can do in terms of making definite progress."

With no other choices available to them, the BMW Team grasped for as much support as those lame straws would bear:

"That's good to know Paul. Thank you for that. I know we are all pulling in the same direction on this and we all want to get the deal closed as soon as we can. Shall we agree to speak later today and you can update us on what Russell King is thinking......say 4.00pm London time".

Yup, we are *in* London after all and I don't need an awful lot of its local time to tell you exactly what Russell King is thinking at the moment.

Russell King was thinking, *"Fuck the lot of you"*; very likely including me.

But we went through all the motions anyway. Setting up the call for later that day; exchanging business cards, letting the faux enthusiasm wash away as much of the hopeless sense of gloom as we could to beguile everyone; everyone that is except the sad, stooped figure of Peter Sauber. He had exactly the measure of Russell King. This deal wasn't going anywhere.

The Taxman

Meanwhile, things had gone from bad to worse at the Football Club.

Russell King telephoned me late in the evening to ring his warning bell:

"I just don't understand how we can owe £530,000 in VAT when we haven't had a gross anything like that figure. Surely 20% of less than £500,000 can't be £530,000".

Well, that sounded right to me. His logic looked impeccable.

"I'll send you over the papers; can you look over them and see what you think? Then have a word with the Revenue and tell them why they have got it all wrong. Richard doesn't know what he is doing. This is way above his head. He keeps calling me to say that we do owe the money and we have to pay. I'm not going to do that until I know that we actually owe this amount".

Richard was the in house accountant. I had last spoken with him on the Saturday of the Formula One deal and he actually seemed pretty competent to me; but there had undoubtedly been a certain frisson between him and Russell King on the call that day and this was likely the reason for it; he was asking the

Club to pay its tax and King couldn't find the money to pay it. Or was it perhaps that the tax claim was overstated (like so much else about Russell King) and the money wasn't due at all; or not in the amount the Revenue was claiming. Even the Inland Revenue sometimes get things wrong. Or so I had been told.

I would have a look at the papers.

These came to all of three pages. The first two were a spreadsheet that Richard had obviously put together. It showed the sales figures for the last two quarters at the Club; broke those down by category and roughed out the VAT to be accounted for. I could see clearly now why King was at daggers drawn with Richard. The calculation showed that there was at least £700,000 due which was *more* than the figure that King had mentioned when he telephoned me earlier in the evening. But there again, that would suggest a gross which was way more than the spreadsheet was recording for the last two quarters; as King had rightly said, VAT had to be accounted for only by reference to the gross sales; so if there was really

£700,000 due, or even the £530,000 that King had told me the Revenue were looking for, then the figures on this sheet were nowhere near enough. But maybe the figures weren't right; and maybe there were VAT arrears due from previous quarters. Maybe the answer would be clear from the third sheet of paper I had been sent by King.

That, as I saw with a shudder, was a letter from the Revenue threatening to bring winding up proceedings for liquidation unless the Club paid £714,000 within the next seven days (four of those had already elapsed; make that three). So the figure Russell King had given me was entirely made up; nothing new there. And the figure supplied by Richard was actually *too little*; but still enough to send Russell King into paroxysms of anger. After a little thought it seemed to me that the easiest way through this, especially with only three days to play with, was also the most pragmatic:

"Pay them what they are asking for Russell. I'll structure the arrangement so that we have these numbers triple checked by a competent accountant and if it turns out that you've have paid too much then the Revenue will refund the excess within seven days. That way the Club doesn't have to get into a life or death fight fending off a winding up petition and it's not as though you don't have the funding to meet the claim."

I mentioned that last point with a certain amount of trepidation. My experience on the Sauber Formula One deal was that King was keen to find any excuse for resisting paying money out (he had made Peter Sauber cry) and something deep inside me, something at a very visceral level, was starting to question whether the money was there at all. That something had not, however, yet hardened into active suspicion. That would not happen for a week or so yet.

"I'm not going to do that Paul, and I'll tell you why. The Revenue are always over inflating claims like this and threatening dire consequences unless they are paid; all this nonsense about winding up petitions and court proceedings. It's all a huge bluff. This football club is a national treasure. They wouldn't dare close it down. I want to call their bluff; I'm not going to pay them anything just because they bark at us loudly and expect us to jump to their command. I want to know exactly how much is due and then I'll pay it. Is that too much to ask?"

"But why take the risk Russell? You have the funding anyway, and I'll make sure the Revenue pay back sharpish anything that is overpaid."

There was that phrase again: *"you have the funding anyway"*. King studiously ignored it and there was now a touch of steel in his voice:

"Don't bully me on this Paul. I wasn't running the Club when this mess was created and all I'm trying to do is to sort out the mess now. Is it really too much to ask that I want to see a proper calculation of the liability before I pay over £530,000 in the hope that the Revenue will be good enough to pay back what isn't actually due? I know what the

216

Revenue are like Paul, they are using bullying tactics and I know for sure that there is nothing like £530,000 due here. Look at the spreadsheet Paul. It just doesn't make any sense."

"They actually want £714,000 Russell."

"What?"

"They want £714,000; not £530,000 Russell."

"What the hell………..

He was angry now

"……£714,000; where are you getting *that* figure from?"

"From the letter you sent me Russell; the letter from the Inland Revenue."

"Jesus. This is all ***bullshi****t*. The claim just keeps going up! I'm not just going to pay them another

217

£200,000 because they decide to ask for it. I want to know what is actually due and then I'll pay it; but I'm not paying *anything* until I know what is properly due. Richard has really fucked this up. I'm not paying anything. Deal with the claim Paul and get me some breathing space so that we can have these figures looked at; as you say, have them looked at by a proper, competent accountant and then we will pay what is actually due. I'm betting on there being nothing due at all. Richard has really fucked this up. Get me some breathing space Paul and I'll deal with it then on the basis of the real figures."

That at least was true. I had told him we should have a competent accountant review the figures and work out what was actually due. But I also thought he was playing Russian roulette with the Club by calling what he fondly described as the Revenue's "bluff". If nothing else, the effect of a winding up petition being issued (just *issued*, not actually determined) would be to freeze the Club's bank accounts, stop dead its credit lines and make all of its creditors (I was assuming there would be lots of them) run for cover and possibly issue proceedings of their own. I knew very little about the economics of running a league football club, but having your bank accounts closed down and losing credit lines across the board seemed a pretty bad outcome to me. I explained all of that to Russell King, trying as gently as I could (he was still angry, in fact getting angrier by the moment) to edge him towards agreeing that I make a more sensible response.

No such luck.

"Look, just sort it out Paul. They can't afford to put this Club out of business; they won't put it out of business. It is the oldest fucking football league club in the world for God's sake."

So I had heard. By now indeed it was becoming a pretty familiar refrain. But I had no doubt that the Revenue would carry through with their threat if they weren't paid. I had a sneaking suspicion though that the VAT claim might even so have been overstated (it was a common ploy, still is, for the Revenue to make an exaggerated claim in order to terrify a taxpayer into a dialogue leading to payment of the correct, or nearly correct, figure). I had one more go with King to get him to engage with reality but it only seemed to anger him more:

"I'm paying **nothing** until I know what is due and I want you to write a letter to Richard with a formal warning that he has fucked this thing up so badly that we are going to have to initiate procedures leading to him being sacked".

That last bit was nonsense of course; but I let it go on the basis King would forget about it pretty quickly during the toing and froing of the inevitable dialogue with the Revenue over the coming days (in fact he didn't).

I just let the call run down; King told me again two or three times that I just had to "sort it out" and he assured me of his immovable belief that if anyone could "sort it out", it was me. I was not so sure.

I called the Revenue the next morning; I hadn't been planning any particular strategy in the meantime, I just wanted an evening off. But the thought of the task ahead had intruded all the same; as these things always did.

The fellow dealing with the matter at the Revenue turned out to have something of a reputation; as well known in his field as Slipper of the Yard was to the Kray Twins. This fellow was charged single handed with the dispatch of all Revenue based insolvency claims against football league clubs; or at least those that the man or woman on the Street would have heard of; Leeds United, those sort of Clubs; and Notts County was about to be added to the notches on his calculating machine unless I could do something within the next (now) two days. He had a certain charm about him albeit mixed with a healthy dose of world weariness so that he always gave the impression of a barber asking you who had cut your hair last time. He was, needless to say, very familiar with the matter:

"Oh yes, I was wondering when someone would call me up about this one."

"Well, as you may know, I'm acting as the solicitor for the Club and I've been asked to talk with you about your letter......"

I picked up the letter so as to refresh my memory

".....your letter of 23 August."

I was waiting for him to say something but he said nothing. He was obviously an old hand at this sort of thing.

".......I saw this for the first time yesterday and obviously it is a matter of concern for the Club; but the fact is that they are still trying to get to grips with the correct figures; you will appreciate that these Returns were posted by the previous management of the Football Club and we aren't wholly sure that they are correct; so it seemed to me, on talking it over yesterday evening, as I say I saw the letter for the first time yesterday, that the best thing to do would be for us to agree a seven day extension of your deadline so that we can get to the bottom of the numbers; then try to agree them with you and, subject to that, whatever needs to be paid can be paid within, say, seven days of signing the accounts off. My client's anxiety is, of course, to meet whatever liability is due, but we have responsibilities to our shareholders as you will appreciate and we can't just pay such a large amount of money without carrying out some due diligence."

I was expecting him to say something during the course of all of that; but instead there was an absolute, stony silence from his end of the line.

"Would that work for you?"

Now there was a sound of shuffling papers before he broke cover:

"£714,000 Mr Fallon; and, let me see, one of those quarters is based on a return that your client's would have prepared so they should already have been in a position to work out what the correct figures were."

I couldn't argue with that:

"Well, I don't want to argue with you on this, but the fact is that the relevant people within the Club have only just seen these figures, as I say I only saw them for the first time last night, and they will need a bit of time to make sure they are correct; at least before making such a substantial payment to you. I'm not sure that is altogether unreasonable".

"But the last return was submitted by *your* client; why would they submit the return if they didn't know whether the figures were right or not?"

That was, I thought, a pretty good point. I was looking at a spreadsheet that had been prepared by the Club's own internal accountant and it showed a figure pretty much on the button with that being demanded by the Revenue. As if he was telepathic, and who am I to say, maybe he was, our Revenue fellow nudged the conversation further along, like a dog nosing a rubber bone:

"Don't you have any internal documents that have been prepared by your own accountants? They ought to be reliable. If you can send me those over and pay what those show now, I will see if we can agree an extra week to decide what else is due and paid".

The spreadsheet prepared by the Club's accountant showed that there was £708,000 due in VAT so sending *that* over to the Revenue wasn't going to be a particular help; certainly Russell King was unlikely to be overjoyed by my having agreed to get him a week to agree how much of the balance of £7,000 should be paid in seven days with £708,000 down the next day. I had an odd feeling that the Revenue knew more about this position than they were letting on. So I followed his example and tried, as all lawyers do from time to time, to make a long silence sound like careful reflection. And the heavens seemed to open up (which to be fair they very rarely do for lawyers so this was something of a surprise):

"Or, let me say this, if Notts County pay £100,000 on account of what is due *tomorrow* I will hold off issuing a winding up petition until the end of the month; but by then, Mr Fallon, we want to see the balance paid off in full or else a cogent reason for persuading us that the figures we have are wrong."

All I had to do was find £100,000 by the following afternoon and the Club were in the clear; at least until the end of the month.

"Well, let me talk to the Club and I'll get back to you tomorrow. I'll see if that might work."

There was, of course, no way that Russell King was going to speak with his paymasters in Bahrain (assuming they existed at all) so as to fund a part payment of £100,000 tomorrow; my conversation with him the previous evening had made that abundantly plain (*very* abundantly plain); but I was thinking that having started the dialogue at Russell King's suggestion, there was no reason why I ought not to seek some sort of affirmation from the Club's directors. Russell King was not, after all, a director of the Club at all. His public position was that he had nothing to do with the day to day operation of the Club. So if I presented what had just happened to one of the Club's directors and tell *him* that within two days the Club would be issued with a winding up petition or, to stave that off, a payment of £100,000 would allow us to put in place a moratorium to the end of the month so that we could work out just how much was actually due by way of VAT.

It might of course be the case that any director of the Club would simply ratify what Russell King had already told me, in which case a winding up petition was bound to follow; but at least they should know what was going on and if they could persuade King, or anyone else for that matter, to cough up the £100,000 then at least we would give the Club a chance to survive. King might not be happy that I was effectively going behind his back; but my client wasn't Russell King. I thought that the Club should be told what was going on and if it had already been told by King then all well and good; if it hadn't and King was annoyed with me for telling them, all well and good too.

So I was feeling a little happier with the position. I knew two directors of the Club who I could contact, Nathan Willett and Peter Trembling. Willett was, of course, far too close to Russell King to act as any sort of neutral sounding board. He had been at the first meeting at the Dorchester with Kevin Leech and he had been the person who had given me instructions to act for Qadbak on the benighted Sauber Formula One transaction. I thought there was more chance of getting Gordon Brown elected than having Nathan Willett toe a different line from Russell King. So Peter Trembling it was. I would call him.

I had met Peter Trembling once or twice already by that stage but it is fair to say that Helen Mulcahy had far more to do with him than I did. He had been the commercial director at Everton Football Club before moving to Notts County with Sven Goran Eriksson. Since the takeover he had been Chief Executive at the Club and, indeed, had travelled to Pyongyang with Sven as part of the SCH delegation in July of that year. Peter had told me when he came back that he had been asked by the North Korean Government to find them a manager who might take charge of their football team for the upcoming 2010 World Cup (where they did pretty well as it happens). He was anguishing over a number of names; Roberto Mancini was one of them as well as Terry Venables (neither of whom took up his offer). Knowing about that exchange and the fact that he had already been out to North Korea on Swiss Commodity business placed him pretty firmly in the Russell King camp in my mind, but I also thought that Trembling was a fair minded and affable fellow (albeit a Scouser) so if anyone was to give the Revenue's proposal a fair hearing it was probably him. I had already decided that there was absolutely no point in going back to Russell King from whom the chances of a fair hearing were precisely zero (let alone getting interim funding of £100,000).

I called Peter Trembling's Office at Meadow Lane and was told that he was in North Korea (again). Writing that now it seems like the most natural thing in the World for a director of a Midlands League Two Football Club to be on business in Pyongyang (again) but those were very different times. Things were simpler then. I had his secretary give me the number of his hotel in Pyongyang. One of the advantages of trying to co-ordinate these negotiations in the afternoon was that I didn't have to wait long for the North Korean morning and, sure enough, by 19.20 London time I had managed to catch Peter Trembling having breakfast at his hotel.

I explained what had happened and it was immediately apparent that Trembling knew nothing about what was happening with the Revenue. But one crucial difference between him on the one hand and King and Willett on the other was that he had invested his future in Notts County. One got every impression from speaking to them that King and Willett could (and indeed later did) drop the Club like a hot brick when it got too hot to handle. But Peter Trembling was different. He was, if nothing else, a football man and he obviously cared about the future of the Club. It was Trembling, indeed, who stepped in at the eleventh hour to orchestrate an attempted takeover of the Club once everything fell apart. He was I think genuinely shocked by the news that the Club would be facing a winding up petition in as little as two and a half days unless its VAT position was regularised.

And unlike Russell King, he obviously knew that the Club could not hope to survive a winding up petition. He was much further down the road than I was as to the reliability of King and Willett and the financial standing of Munto and Qadbak. I suppose it should have struck me in particular, although it certainly didn't do so at the time, that he was inevitably much closer to the heart of the SCH/North Korean transactions than I was. For one thing he was talking to me from North Korea. He also dealt much more regularly than I did with King and Willett and was in a better position to test their truthfulness than I was. He told me a lot on that call which gave me cause to stop and think. He told me, for example, that the Club had stopped paying its milk bill so no more milk was being delivered to Meadow Lane; it had also stopped paying its Opta Player Performance suppliers (pretty much an essential supply for any modern football club) and it had stopped paying his own wages for at least the past month. He was, it seems, travelling to North Korea on the basis of a promise that missed wages today would be more than made up for by SCH shares tomorrow (a fiction that Sven Goran Eriksson had also bought into). In any event, Peter Trembling wasn't surprised to hear that the Club was facing a Revenue Petition for unpaid VAT; neither did he disagree with me that there was no point in asking Russell King to fund the suggested interim payment of £100,000. Not least because the milkman had been asking Trembling for much smaller payments without any success for at least two months. None of that looked or felt, of course, like a Club with multi million (if not billion) pound backing from a Middle Eastern State.

Trembling and I agreed instead that he would fund the £100,000 interim from funds which my Firm were holding in escrow to his account. He would then arrange to be paid later back for the sum advanced as though it were a loan made on behalf of the Club. Quite why he agreed to do that bearing in mind what he must have known about King and Willett at that time, only some of which he had told me during the course of the call, I just don't know. But he did and I think on balance that this was to his credit because, as I have said, more than anyone else involved in this story, Peter Trembling had the good of the Club at heart; he wanted the Notts County project to succeed and virtually alone amongst those who were directly involved with the Club, he was prepared to put his money where his mouth is.

So I arranged to transfer the funds to the Revenue first thing the following morning and the Club got the breathing space that it needed; although not ultimately enough to matter because sooner or later the absence of any substantial funding such as that promised by

King and Willett was bound to show through. In the words of Warren Buffett, when the tide goes out you find out who is wearing a swimming costume. We were just waiting for the tide to go out, that was all; and no matter how generous and no matter how misguided Peter Trembling was in making payments to stave off disaster in the meantime, the tide *was* bound to go out.

King and Willett were seemingly doing all they could to hasten natural processes. One of their signings of the summer, Sol Campbell, had not found Meadow Lane to be all that he thought it would be. He was making very public grumblings about the quality of the changing rooms and training facilities and these were taking away some of the glister from the Project which Sven and others were trying to counteract in the press (mostly without any success – as any journalist will know, happiness writes white in any event). Sol Campbell only turned out once for the Club, for a rain smitten away game against Morecambe Town which Notts County lost. It seems to have been the last straw for him. His grumblings grew in pitch and ferocity and eventually he left the Club altogether; without giving any notice and without telling anyone where he was going. *Anywhere but Meadow Lane* would have been the rational answer had he bothered to say. To add to that David Beckham had decided not after all to join the Club, which was a bit of a downer for all concerned, and (in common with the milkman) some of the players, including Kasper Schmeichel, had started not to be paid at the end of the week. It was not a particularly potent recipe for success.

I spoke with Russell King after the payment to the Revenue had been made; it was fair to say that he was not chuffed but what was he going to say? The Club had been a matter of days away from ceasing to exist; why would it be a matter for critical comment that anyone should have taken steps to prevent it shaking hands with the infinite? So when I spoke with him he was not overtly puckish, as was his usual demeanour; rather he was dry and rather arch in telling me that he agreed (as I had suggested to him the previous day) that we should retain some independent accountants to take a look at the paperwork and find out if there were errors that needed to be corrected. We could use that process to give us some leverage also against the Revenue; it would help to say that there had been a change of ownership and whatever the legacy problems left behind by the old owners, we were doing our very best to clean them up. That should help us to buy some time. Or at least I hoped it would.

I recommended to King that we should involve a small time accountant that I knew (small time meant cheap and I knew that would appeal to Russell); Paul Smethurst sounded like just the right fellow. We scheduled a conference call at which Russell King could, and did, sound off about the uselessness of the Club's in house accounts function (Richard was sacked two weeks later) and I explained the timeline we would have to work to; the Revenue had only given the Club until the end of the month to pay up the rest of the £600,000 which they had demanded failing which we would have to be in a position to point to concrete evidence demonstrating that the amount they had demanded in the first place was too high. Smethurst was as pleased as a Cheshire cat and in no time at all he had settled on a code name for the Project: *Project Robin Hood* they called it; no doubt because the Club was in Nottingham but perhaps to reflect the fact that Russell King was robbing everybody to pay himself.

Smethurst duly sent a team of his accountants down to the Club's Meadow Lane offices that weekend and they worked flat out, or at least they said they did; accountants rarely adopt any other posture while working. I heard very little about what they were actually getting up to or what they were finding until the Wednesday of the following week when King called me again; there was a weary sense of history repeating itself:

"Paul, these accountants you have retained for this exercise; they're useless. I keep trying to get them to concentrate on the facts that matter but they have no sense of focus; they are ranging over all the books, running up a fortune in fees and they are adding no value at all. They won't listen to me."

"I'm sorry to hear that Russell. What do you want to do about it?"

"I think you should sack them."

"*I* should sack them. Why me?"

"Because you were the one who brought them in."

That seemed to me to be a little rich. But I did, and then they sued us for their unpaid fees. I added that to the pile of Milbank Tweed invoices.

The Football League

This was all a very a potent recipe to attract the attention of any regulator; and it duly did, in this case the Football League.

We had received a letter, precipitated no doubt by the story that the *Sun* had run about Russell King's insurance frauds, asking for clarification on the ownership structure of the Club; and also for clarification as to just who was involved in its day to day management. The individuals in question would all be required to submit applications so as to satisfy the fitness and propriety tests operated by the Football League. They would have to demonstrate that they were fit and proper persons to be involved in the operation of a Football League Club; and quite right too, Notts County was, after all, the oldest Football League Club in the World.

We had already told the League in the fallout of the Aston Martin Insurance Frauds that Russell King had no involvement of any kind in the day to day operations of the Club. It is fair to say that the League's compliance team were treating that assurance with more than a grain of salt; but as we had also told King (as had the Club) not to be seen at Meadow Lane and to make no statements of any kind, public or private, in connection with its affairs, it would be difficult for them to say that he did any longer have any relevant involvement. In fairness I don't think he did; but with such a devious and untrustworthy individual, looking back who can say. I believe on balance that the compliance team were right to remain sceptical.

It was one thing to say who was *not* involved in the day to day management of the Football Club; quite another to say who <u>was</u> running Notts County. As the days unwound, that was to prove the pivotal question. Of course we knew that Nathan Willett and Peter Trembling were board members and very much did exercise day to day control over the operations of the Club; but it was obvious too that neither of them had the financial wherewithal to fund the Club's projected business so there was no option other than to try to dig into the corporate structure as well; it was a no brainer that whoever was funding the operations of the Club must be having some say in what the Club was doing day to day. That presumably was what they were paying their money for. They were funding the Notts County Project. But who were *they*?

I went into session with Nathan Willett to find out. He had already told me about Qadbak, but he was very quick to tell me as well that Qadbak had nothing to do with either the ownership or the operation of Notts County. Instead he pointed to the British Virgin Islands Company, Munto Finance which was in turn owned by Qadbak Investments Ltd. Munto, he said, owned 99.9% of the issued shares in Notts County. So who then owned Qadbak Investments? Willett said he didn't know but that he would find out. I asked him whether it was Russell King or anyone associated with Russell King (that obviously being the disaster scenario as far as Football League compliance was concerned) but he assured me it wasn't. He was right about that. It wasn't Russell King at all.

Qadbak Investments was owned, we were told, by a Middle Eastern potentate by the name of Anwar Shafi. Willett produced that information to me as though he were divulging the codes to a Bullion Vault. Even so, and whilst obviously I was prepared to give such due deference to what Willet told me as it was worth, I still thought it would be sensible for me to speak with Mr Shafi to verify the nature of his ownership interest in Qadbak Investments. There was a good deal of shuffling of feet from Willett's side at that suggestion. He would be difficult to contact; always on the move; a secretive chap who wouldn't value a London lawyer nosing around in his affairs; all of that usual stuff.

But still I persisted.

What I wound up with subsequently was an e-mail from Shafi saying he was the Founder of the Qadbak Trust which had settled the assets of the Foundation on members of the Hyat and Shafi families and these Family Members, through their discretionary holdings in the Foundation, were the true owners (or the nearest thing we had to owners) of the shares in Qadbak Investments Ltd and, through that company, to Munto Investments Ltd and, through the Club's immediate holding company Blenheim 1885, to the Club itself. I also had an opportunity to talk on a particularly bad phone line with Anwar Shafi himself who was able to confirm everything that I had been told in his e-mail. At least I was told that it was Anwar Shafi. The Club seemed almost as pleased to hear about this as I was because they almost immediately posted a statement on their website saying that Shafi and members of his and the Hyat families were the ultimate owners of the Club.

It was all very complicated but it would do. We put together a series of structure charts and written declarations for each of the individuals who had been identified (except the Sharif family members who, we said, could not be expected to sign declarations given their interests in the Foundation were entirely discretionary). That was all then polished up and put into a lever arch file and sent off to the Football League's Headquarters at Gloucester Place in London. We also included a rather more emphatic declaration than had so far been given saying that Russell king had absolutely nothing to do with the day to day running of Notts County. Honest. So far so good.

But an immediate spanner was thrown into the works.

On 6 October 2009 we received draft copy from the *Guardian* Newspaper with the text of a story saying that their journalist, Matt Scott (a regular thorn in the side of the Club) had been in contact with Anwar Shafi and he had told Matt Scott that:

"It's not me. This Statement was not made by me. I have no investment of any sort in Qadbak. I have no role in the Club."

Shafi also told the Newspaper that representatives of Qadbak had contacted him during recent weeks (no doubt I was one of them) and attempted to recruit him "with a view to employment as a spokesperson or with an ambassadorial role" but that he had turned them down. If that was true then it was news to me.

But it got even worse than that. The story went on to say that far from being the Middle Eastern potentate that he had been presented to me, Anwar Shafi in fact ran a small factory outside Islamabad in Pakistan making paving stones. He said that he had travelled to Bahrain the previous month and had met with Russell

King (him again) and had been offered "millions of dollars in shares" to become an ambassador for Qadbak but had turned the offer down. He was quoted as saying that he was "shocked" to learn of the announcement on the Notts County website and had learned about it only through a friend who had searched the site four days after the announcement was posted. The Paper went on:

"Shafi laughed at the description of the Shafi and Hyat families as fabulously rich with extensive international business interests. *We are prominent families of the Indian sub-continent and specifically Punjab. But we are not tycoons, not even in Pakistan*".

We were due to meet with the League's compliance team only two days after this story was scheduled to appear (it was to come out the next day). Plainly some damage limitation was called for. After working with Willett and speaking with Hardar Hyat (or at least I was told it was him) during the course of the day and into the early evening, the Hyat Family Trust (yet another entity) was able to issue a Press release saying that it was shocked by the story and *"condemns any attempt to interpret their wish to continue to conduct their business affairs with discretion and privacy as in some way hallmarked by an intention to deceive the public as to the nature of the interests in the underlying family trust and the companies in its ownership. The family are well aware of the operations of Qadbak and its interest in Notts County Football Club and have never sought to conceal that interest from anyone"*.

In fairness, the Guardian printed the text of that release word for word the next day as part of its story. But I didn't think we were fooling anyone and spent the rest of the day in an uneasy frame of mind preparing for the meeting at the Football League's Headquarters the next day. I had arranged to meet Peter Trembling there. He was to act as the public face of the Club in its meetings with the League and its compliance committee; my job was to persuade it that there was a clear and obvious chain of ownership and that every relevant person in the chain was a fit and proper person to be involved in the running of an English football League Club. In my own mind I thought that task had become virtually impossible in the light of the story run by the *Guardian* earlier that day.

What self-respecting compliance officer could possibly accept that the ultimate owner of Qadbak Investments (and through it the Club) was a family trust structure which the supposed settlor of the trust had apparently never heard of, but which was also supposedly being run by someone making paving stones in Islamabad?

Was it even conceivable that the Football League would give a green light to any of that?

I took a call from Nathan Willett on the morning the *Guardian* Article appeared; unlike me, he thought it was not particularly damaging (which, if nothing else, seemed to call into question the quality of his instincts as the director of a limited liability company). He was in a buoyant frame of mind but thought that Peter

Trembling, who would be required to attend the next day's meeting at Football League Headquarters, was beginning to wilt under the strain of the whole thing. He asked whether I could meet with him later that day so as to stiffen his resolve and brief him on what to say.

That was fine by me. I had never met him face to face before but I knew that he had already stepped into the breach to help out with the looming disaster that was the Inland Revenue; so, in short, I thought he deserved all the help that we could give him. As I have said, I thought he was in general a good sort and of course I could well understand that given the tone of the *Guardian*'s Article he could well be falling prey to self-doubt about the whole Notts County Project.

We were to meet at Chelsea Football Club's ground at Stamford Bridge in West London. Along with the rest of the great and the good of English Football, Peter Trembling was attending for their Annual Conference. The likely outcome of the next day's meeting at the Football League was obviously a hot issue at the conference so when I arrived there it was no surprise to find Trembling in the middle of a televised interview with Sky Sports; as we hadn't met before he obviously didn't recognise me as I sidled up to the edge of the small crowd listening to him being grilled on who was running Notts County (as if any of us actually knew). It was an odd experience listening to the press release that I had drafted the previous evening being reeled out by him effortlessly in answer to even the most awkward questions; I found myself almost believing what he was saying:

"…….and what about Russell King? We heard a lot both from him and about him in the early days of the takeover. What is his present position at the Club Peter? Can you tell us something about that?"

There was no hesitation at all in his answer:

"Russell King has nothing whatsoever to do with the day to day operations of the Club. I am the Chief Executive Officer at Notts County and along with the other members of the Board; we are responsible for the day to day operations of the Club. Russell King has no influence on anything, nothing at all, that either I or any of my fellow directors are doing at the Club".

That was a pretty good answer. I couldn't have scripted it better myself; but there again, I had scripted it. But he seemed to be doing pretty well. I was thinking that Nathan Willett's concerns, as expressed to me by telephone that morning, were probably ill founded.

The interviewer was visibly trying to keep his microphone from shaking in the chill drizzle of the rain that had been falling most of the day. I held my position like Polonius behind the Arras. It did cross my mind to wonder what I would do if he was asked a particularly devastating question; would my duties to the Club require me to interrupt the interview and protect him; especially bearing in mind that whatever he was saying now would no doubt find its way rapidly into the hands of the compliance team at the

Football League who would be grilling us tomorrow. Happily, I never had to formulate a plan on that front because Trembling was doing just fine:

"…..and can you help us understand who exactly does own Notts County. Like us, you will have seen the article in the Guardian this morning; taken at face value it looks as though the person that the Club itself put forward on its own website as the representative of the owners says he knows nothing about who they are; the article suggests that he may have been wrongly quoted on that. Do you have anything to say about that Peter?"

Good question.

"Well, these are issues that the Football League will be looking into at tomorrow and it is all in the hands of the Club's lawyers so I probably shouldn't say anything in advance of that save that I have no reason to question what the Club has said on its website".

Another good answer; for the time being at least.

Things went on in much the same vein for a few minutes more before the interview then descended into football gossip, save that there were still one or two acid drop questions about why Sol Campbell seemed not to be happy at Meadow Lane. Trembling dealt with those well too.

After they had wrapped up, and after leaving a little time for Trembling to chat with the people at Sky before they packed up (I did not, of course, want to rush over immediately and say *"Hi Peter I'm the Club's lawyer"*, which could have led to me being interviewed as well), I edged out and introduced myself. He seemed pleased to meet me after the Korean telephone conversation.

I explained that Willett had asked me to come along to see him to make sure he was coping with everything and I also told him that I would be coming along to the League meeting tomorrow to make the formal presentation to their compliance team. He seemed very visibly relieved to hear that and, indeed, was keen to suggest that if I would be attending the meeting then there was really no need for him to go along as well.

I disillusioned him on that one.

In my experience it is not, save in unusual circumstances, sensible to meet with any regulatory body for a substantial matter without having a senior member of the client present. That is especially so where issues of ownership, fitness and propriety are in question (as of course they would be tomorrow). It is important then to demonstrate to the regulator that the client is interested enough in the process to bother sending a senior executive along to the meeting (rule 1) and that the senior executive in question is demonstrably fit and proper himself (rule 2). I did once have an executive who decided to attend a regulatory meeting with me in wide pinstriped suit, black shirt and white tie looking for all the world like a nineteen thirties bank robber, but that was an exception that proves the rule. Peter Trembling was much more of a salt of the earth sort of chap and I was keen to have him with me tomorrow to demonstrate that the higher echelons of Notts County were not filled with people like Russell King (which indeed, in substantial part at least, they weren't).

Trembling took his blocked escape route in good heart.

He suggested that we might try to find Lord Triesman who was attending the Conference and who was, at that time, a high ranking member of the Football League. It might be worth talking to him. So we set off inside; Peter got through easily with his enormous laminated pass which hung like an albatross from his neck; for my part, as a "privileged guest" I had to go through all of the security checks one would expect at an international airport which stopped only (just) short of an anal probe. I bore all of that with fortitude. It seemed to me only to be expected in the rarefied and glamorous world of association football.

Things were, though, far from glamorous inside. It was just like any other antiseptic convention centre; this time seeming to have been hastily assembled in an enormous tent stuck onto the side of Chelsea's football ground. Groups of disconsolate looking delegates were either sitting half a dozen to each of the many melamine tables assembled round the floor or else milling glumly between the tables like characters from Dante in search of someone to speak with.

And they all seemed to know Peter Trembling. He was slapped on the back and shaken by the hand by almost everyone that he came within reach of; including, as I remember, the piping voiced pit-bull that is Garth Crooks (who up until then I had seen only on *Match of the Day* with my children); Garth assured Trembling and me that the meeting tomorrow would go fine. So did everybody else. I was almost starting to believe them. Almost.

And so we milled and milled around the floor for a good twenty minutes, Trembling being consoled and heartened, before we finally met with Lord Triesman.

He was an imposing enough character but his qualities were veiled to a certain extent because, at least as it seemed to me, he had had rather too much to drink. He was sweating ferociously (which might, to be fair, have been a result of the drizzle and the heat and all the hot air inside) and his bonhomie seemed to swamp his sense of the occasion; particularly our occasion tomorrow. So we made do with his prediction, like Garth Crooks and the others, that everything would go fine tomorrow; he was sure. In any event there was nothing else that he needed from us so we made do with what we could get on that front.

I left Trembling to it and went back to my office to prepare for the meeting tomorrow.

The Regulatory Grilling

As I drove over to Gloucester Place the next morning I was listening to a sports programme on the car radio; broadcast by *"Talk Sport"*, its presenter was making scathing comments about the public comments attributed to Anwar Shafi by Notts County; that it was time for the Football League to act responsibly and to call for greater transparency from ownership interests and clear evidence of their financial standing. I actually agreed with that and I was mentally preparing to answer exactly the same questions when we sat down with the compliance committee half an hour later.

When I got there I found that the Football League at least had an impressive suite of meeting rooms. Despite its then recent travails with ITV, it was plainly running over with cash; photographs of its sporting icons (I couldn't see anyone from Notts County) were hung floor to ceiling and its trophies, including oddly the Premier League Trophy, were lit like works of art in their tubular glass cases. I was examining the Premier League Trophy, mostly because I have two football oriented children, when I caught a glimpse of Peter Trembling out of the corner of my eye. I thought it would be bad form to leave him to continue to tussle alone with the great and the good of the League so I made my way over.

He was talking with Brian Mawhinney, Chairman of the Football League; Lord Mawhinney, former Conservative Government Minister and, as it happens, former lecturer in medical physics at the Royal Free School of medicine where my ex-wife trained as a doctor:

"You taught my wife medical physics at the Royal Free in 1980",

I made the point in fairly friendly fashion although I was very aware that my ex-wife hated the man and he was indeed also something of a hate figure in our family at large; he was the MP for my brother's constituency in Peterborough and my brother despises all Conservative MP's. But I was being nice to Lord Mawhinney this morning (for obvious reasons).

He smiled at that; surprisingly pleasantly (at least *I* was surprised given all the terribly bad things I had heard about him over the years); he smiled, shook my hand warmly and said:

"I hope she doesn't hold that against me".

"I'm not sure; I think she might rather."

He smiled again.

He thought I was joking, but I wasn't:

"But I hope you won't take exception to the whole family. I'm here on behalf of Notts County Football Club so I'm hoping for a level playing field".

I looked over at Peter Trembling while I said that; he looked terrified.

"I know you have a lot on your plate today so I hope we won't be adding to your burden unduly".

That was true. In addition to the ownership position at Notts County, the League were also reviewing the fitness and propriety of the then owner of Queens Park Rangers Football Club (Brigatone had recently been expelled from the F1 Association, appropriately enough bearing in mind my very recent dealings with Bernie Ecclestone, as a result of tax evasion convictions; could he, one asked, continue to be fit and proper to run a football club if he was not fit and proper to own and operate a formula one racing team; who knew?) Then the League was also to deal with Leeds United. So I was hoping that Mawhinney and his team would have so much on their plates that they wouldn't notice our little peccadillos, paving stone salesmen and convicted insurance fraudsters. His Lordship's trademark politician smile gave me cause for hope.

"Nothing that we can't handle, I'm sure".

Mawhinney beamed back at me.

"I'm sure everything will be OK, nothing to worry about; the compliance team will look after you upstairs".

He was ushering us away now, towards the meeting suite.

It seemed odd to me then and it still seems odd to me now that the Football League, not exactly a low profile and underfunded organisation, should have conspired so to arrange for three of its hottest compliance issues to be dealt with, and as it turned out to be rushed through, on the same day. They were none of them exactly straightforward and in my own experience any properly modulated compliance function would look to consider the facts carefully and to moderate its findings through a process of careful consultation and drafting. Far from that, it appeared from what Peter Trembling was now telling me that the Football League were planning to finalise its deliberations on *all three* matters during the course of a single day and to announce its decisions that same evening. So far as Notts County were concerned, they had only been sent the file of information they had requested and we had prepared some three days earlier; and they had been sent it in the immediate context of the most unfavourable national press comment that I could imagine. Why then was Lord Mawhinney flashing us his winning smile and telling us he was sure that everything would be alright?

The "compliance team" turned out to be a team of two; neither of whom looked as though they were in any sense the sharpest knife (or indeed anything else) in the box. They had obviously received the lever arch file I had put together earlier in the week because there it was in front of them on the desk; and like Lord Mawhinney downstairs they were sweetness and light up here too. It was hard to tell whether either of them had actually read the file of papers we had sent, as opposed to skim through it (I am sure at least one of them had skimmed the papers) but they had each certainly read the *Guardian* article; in fact they seemed pretty chuffed that their matter had made it into the papers:

"You'll have seen all of this stuff in the papers about the pavement man in Pakistan. We aren't really interested in any of that because no-one is saying that he is actually the owner of Notts County are they?"

"Well I'm certainly not. He's the spokesman for the Family Trusts; administered on behalf of the Hyat and Shafi families. I'm sure you will have read through that in the file I sent over".

I nodded casually at the file as I said this which was a cue for one of them to open it up and skim the opening section; riffling the pages like a schoolboy with a pack of cards; but not actually, and very obviously, not *actually* reading any of them.

"No, of course; thank you very much for sending this over Paul. It's very helpful".

"It's our pleasure. These things tend to acquire a head of steam of their own with such ill-informed press speculation; things are difficult enough for Peter here........"

I flapped an idle hand to indicate Peter Trembling sitting next to me – still palpably terrified but beginning to unfreeze a little; I think, like me, he was beginning to see a little cause for hope; they were being so friendly and receptive; I half expected to be offered a tray of sandwiches with the crusts cut off.

".....They are difficult enough for Peter here, I am sure he never dreamed when he took over as Chief Executive at the Club that he would have to put up with this kind of nonsense. He has, I can assure you, been working day and night not only to deal with idle press speculation of the kind you mentioned, but to keep the Club running smoothly in the most difficult circumstances".

By which I meant, of course, Russell King but I didn't say so; the subject of King was bound to come up of its own accord in a moment. I was busy painting Peter Trembling as a martyr to English football; a true, black and white striped Notts County martyr. He duly assumed the face and demeanour of a martyr; eyes cast down and exuding the pains of his office. He was quite impressive.

"So I can tell you without any qualification this morning that there is no truth whatsoever in the suggestions put forward by the *Guardian* this week that the finances of the Club have no substantial basis. You have in your file statements and structure charts from and about the Hyat and Shafi Families; you will see that the ownership structures are very clearly set out and explained; the one point you will not see in any detail in the file (but it is explained in sufficient outline terms in the overview section at tab 1), is an in depth explanation of the individual financial circumstances of each of the Hyat and Shafi family members who are beneficiaries under the Family Trusts; and the reason for that, as I hope you will understand, is because these people are *discretionary* beneficiaries. They have an interest under the trust but the nature of that interest, because it is discretionary, means they are entitled, and I am not using that word lightly, they are entitled to preserve their privacy and family circumstances; whatever the journalists at the *Guardian* and other members of the yellow press might or might not think otherwise."

I was expecting to be interrupted by then so I paused; half out of a sense of relief that I hadn't been; half to give them a chance to. But they said nothing. It seemed they were actually swallowing this nonsense.

"You see, we believe quite strongly that whilst any regulator, including you, has an obligation to ensure that standards of fitness and propriety are properly regulated and enforced, there is a point where legitimate expectations of privacy take over; it is incumbent on us, as the Club is a regulated entity, to make plain to you what the ownership structure is; and to answer your questions without any equivocation, because you are obviously entitled, and indeed obliged, to require us to do that; but where, as here, the interests comprise in part open and absolute interests and in part discretionary trust interests, you have to draw a line in the interests of fairness between the two; you cannot cross into the discretionary sector because that would be to interfere in the legitimate expectations that the discretionary beneficiaries have to a private family life. I hope you understand that......."

I looked hard at the two of them; they seemed to be thinking things over so I rammed the point home as best I could:

"........Whatever the *Guardian* or the Tabloid Press at large might otherwise think. These are issues of fairness and natural justice. We have answered all of your questions and given all the information we can with those constraints in mind."

If they didn't go for that we were screwed. I held my breath. I'm not sure Peter Trembling understood what I had said or, indeed, the significance of the point; but if only out of a sense of good team work he seemed to be holding his breath too.

"Yes, of course; we do accept that Paul. The papers are certainly in order on that; we can't tell you so for certain now but for the moment we don't think there is anything else we will need from you for the moment. There was though just one thing…….."

I could feel my teeth clench; this was where it would all fall apart then.

"I take it that Russell King no longer has any involvement in the day to day operations at Notts County? You haven't mentioned him in the structure chart on page two. I think we need confirmation on that point in the light of the press last month."

He was talking, of course, about the Aston Martin insurance fraud.

"Of course. Russell King has nothing at all to do with the operations of the Club and that has been the position since the end of October when we found out about his full track record. You're right to ask, sorry; I should have made that clear in the file itself but I wanted to concentrate on those who were actually involved in the operation of the Club rather than those who weren't".

"Of course, I understand that Paul. But thank you for confirming the point".

"Not at all. I can tell you that Peter Trembling here had an appalling time trying to deal with him, so he is probably the happiest of anyone here finally to see the back of Russell King."

Trembling adopted again his early Christian martyr look. He was doing a pretty good job of that.

"Understood; I just thought we'd ask Paul, but thank you for confirming the position and thank you both too for taking the time out to come in to see us today".

And that was it. It was all over in five or at most six minutes. The sharp toothed watchdog of propriety at the Football League seemed to have its rubber dentures in; both sets of them. So we spent another twenty minutes or so talking about my sons' keen interest in Manchester United and Norwich City (where the facts at least were more plausible than the bullshit I had spent the last five minutes spouting); Peter Trembling was commiserated on his martyr status for English football (and again dropped his eyes and grimaced to signify the stigmata he bore); and then we were being told that they would report to their executive that day and we would hear from them with a final decision within a day or so. I offered to provide them with any further information they might need as part of that process but I had no expectation that they would actually ask for anything; their minds seemed to be pretty much made up and it looked as though we were in the clear.

Now, I have dealt over the years with a number of regulatory bodies; including the Financial Services Authority, the Bank of England, the Department of Trade and, most memorable, the full terrors of the Securities and Exchange Commission in the United States; and none of them, least of all the Securities and Exchange Commission, were in my experience particularly docile or especially susceptible to being beguiled by the routine smoke and mirrors of legal presentation. Whatever the general public might think, regulators as a whole do a pretty good job of weeding out those who are involved in the disreputable shadow play of impropriety.

But I would make an exception for the Football League.

As a regulator it had all the utility of a chocolate teapot. During the course of my dealings with its compliance function, I found them to be constantly wading out of their depth; seeming to be utterly star struck by the routine glamour of the world of football of which they thought themselves kings and, ironically in the circumstances, constantly taking their eye off the ball and playing the man. I have little if any doubt but that the *Guardian* had, back then in 2009, got the facts right and had taken the true pulse of the question: the ownership structure of Notts County was so opaque and so convoluted that it was simply impossible to say who was actually running the operation; and if you couldn't even say who was running it, then how on earth could you say that they were fit and proper persons to be involved in a football club at all? No competent regulator would allow itself to be painted into such a corner but from what I had heard as I left the meeting that seemed to be exactly what was now going to happen. At the time it seemed too good to be true. Now it seems to me to be entirely risible.

The powers that be at the Football League were acting like rank amateurs.

As we were leaving the meeting suite we ran into Lord Mawhinney again. He smiled his toothsome smile:

"So how did it all go Peter? They weren't too ferocious with you I hope."

He said this as he shook Trembling's hand with surprising vigour.

Peter Trembling, for his part, seemed to have regained some of his composure:

"Yes, thanks very much Brian. It went well I think. What do you think Paul?"

His entire martyr demeanour seemed to have seeped away now and he was looking at me with the air of a dog who seeks forgiveness for pooping on the carpet.

"Yes, I think it went well Peter but we'll have to wait for Lord Mawhinney and his executive to look things over so we won't count our chickens just yet."

"Oh, I'm sure it will be fine", boomed his Lordship, repeating the refrain he had left us with thirty minutes ago which all sounded encouraging. Indeed, he now seemed to be much more interested in Trembling's preservation from the yellow press:

"There are quite a few photographers and cameramen out the front of the building, just so you know Peter. It's best to be forewarned about these things."

He was speaking with the practiced air of a politician who had undoubtedly run the gauntlet of press interest much more often than Peter Trembling or I had. Trembling obviously shared the concern for his preservation:

"Oh, I see. There were some there this morning as well; and journalists asking a few questions. I'd prefer to avoid having to go through that again if I could. Is there a back way out of the building that I could use to try to avoid them?"

And indeed there was; out by the bins into the carpark and up a steel staircase to the street. We were given appropriate directions by his Lordship and then Peter Trembling and I, like Elvis, left the building.

Even when we were chatting by the bins, his sense of encirclement never left Peter; he told me that he thought it would be for the best if we left via the steel staircase separately because it might look odd if I was recognised as a lawyer and he had thought it necessary to come to the meeting with one. I doubted that was right, for a start it was massively unlikely anyone would recognise me as a lawyer; but I deferred to his sense of siege and so stayed waiting by the bins as Trembling made his way out alone back onto the street. He looked very isolated and I hoped there would be brighter days ahead at the Club now that Russell king had been carved free of its operations.

As if to cast doubt on my hopes, it started to drizzle lightly.

After waiting for exactly five minutes, which I thought was a seemly delay allowing for the fact that Trembling might have been accosted by journalists even at the back door, I made my way up the stairs and onto the street. There was nobody there. Peter seemed, for the time being at least, to have given them the slip.

The Decision

We didn't have to wait long for a decision.

That very evening Sky News carried a report that Notts County had met its *"fit and proper persons regulations"* and that whilst the ownership structure at the Club was *"complicated"* and featured both *"offshore entities and discretionary trusts"* it had provided *"extensive documentation"* to the League on its ownership structure and that public disclosure as to the full details of that ownership structure was essentially a matter for the Club; it was not a matter for its Regulator.

I had been led to expect that there would be a favourable outcome to the day; from the snippets and suggestions dropped by the League's compliance team and, indeed, by Lord Mawhinney himself; but I was surprised that the outcome had been determined so soon; within the course of a single afternoon. Many of the Regulatory matters that I had been involved in in the past had taken weeks and sometimes months to resolve following presentation of our submissions. It was almost as though they had made their minds up before Peter Trembling and I had even set foot in their meeting suite; but surely that couldn't be the case.

Then there was the reference in the decision to our having supplied the League with *"extensive documentation"*. It was true that if they were used to receiving a slim sheaf of paper to justify ownership interests then the lever arch file which we had given them was indeed extensive. But for the most part it was comprised of google searches and public information of the most asinine kind. Deliberately so; we had to "bulk it up" somehow. But the information was far from extensive and, in the light of the warning bells sounded by the *Guardian* in the very week of the meeting, I was to say the least, surprised that the papers had not only passed muster but in some way were thought to be comprehensive; which they were not. Indeed, I strongly suspected that those entrusted with reviewing the information had done nothing more than skim through the file; it was hard otherwise to explain the behaviour of the compliance team at the meeting.

But of course I was happy. The Club had come through its ordeal with flying colours. I sent a congratulatory e-mail to Peter Trembling but never heard back from him. He was one of those folk, I suspected, who only talk to lawyers when they need them. I didn't mind. In any event we were to hear from him when he needed us next; a couple of weeks later.

What I didn't understand at the time, but appreciate now, is that the formulation of the Football League's decision that day was not really intended for the Club, still less my Firm, at all. It was directed to the public at large who took an interest in what the League were doing; the sort of people who might have read the *Guardian* article with interest. And in addressing that particular constituency, it was clearly important that the League should give the impression that it had conducted a thorough and exhaustive inquiry; that was why it had stated, quite misleadingly, that the Club had provided it with "extensive information" on its ownership structure when in fact it had done nothing of the kind. And, of course, it could rely on a silent conspiracy to keep the fiction in place because neither I; my firm, nor anyone at the Club was about to blow the whistle and say that the information supplied had been, particularly in context, laughably thin.

But there we are. The fiction of compliance was at least created and it held together for all of a month before the League woke up to the poverty of its procedures.

The *Guardian* ran another article on 27 November of 2009; it reported, correctly as it happens, that the

League had re-opened its inquiries into the ownership structure at the Club. I knew about that because the previous week the League had sent the Club a far more extensive written request asking for information and papers on the ownership interests; so extensive indeed that I could see no way that we could possibly answer it with the kind of generic nonsense that the League had swallowed the previous month. Willett had already been on the telephone on a number of occasions to suggest I *"spirit something up"*. I wasn't about to start doing that and had, for the first time, heard something of his naked aggression in response. We weren't, in short, getting on too well. I suspect someone at the League or the Club had leaked the fact that this latest request for information had met with complete silence. People were obviously drawing their own inferences.

More worryingly, however, the *Guardian* had also started to ask questions about the terms of the guarantee which First London had provided to Blenheim so as to secure the purchase of the Club in the first place; without that guarantee it was highly unlikely that the supporters club would have signed over control of the Club for a nominal consideration of £1. The guarantee was anything but a guarantee; it contained none of the conventional assurances that a Bank might offer in similar circumstances and it could be called on only when a creditor had obtained a Court Judgement against the Club and the Judgement had remained unsatisfied following execution (by a bailiff or bankruptcy for example). If a judgement was unsatisfied in those circumstances the Club would be hopelessly bust anyway and the guarantee would be redundant. That was why I had been uneasy to learn that Helen Mulcahy had relied on just this document to demonstrate to the League the previous month that the Club was solvent. It was, of course, no evidence of anything of the kind (as Helen Mulcahy should have known). The *Guardian* wasn't mincing its words:

"The letter of guarantee is drafted in an unconventional fashion and may not be easily enforceable. An expert in contract law has raised doubts about the document. A corporate law partner at Olswang has said: *'the letter of guarantee is quite imprecise and confusing.........the breadth of the wording regarding settlement would imply that [the Club] would have to seek final legal judgement against Munto before it could secure funds from First London. This is unusual."*

I couldn't have put it better myself.

As with the previous *Guardian* article, this one had been put together by an investigative journalist on its sports desk who went by the name of *the Digger;* he was called that, I assume, either because he liked digging or because he did a lot of digging, either explanation would have been appropriate because whatever he did he dug. He was a fellow called Matt Scott and it is fair to say that his repeated digging was not making him any friends at Meadow Lane. He wasn't exactly flavour of the month at First London either especially as this article, for the first time, was casting doubt on the standing, or at least the financial reliability, of First London itself. Why would a reputable bank enter into an instrument in such unconventional terms? Didn't it suggest that the bank itself was unconventional to the point of disreputable?

That was another problem altogether.

As with the first of the *Guardian* articles we had been sent proof copy the night before and had been invited to comment on the accuracy of what they were saying. In the light of what they were proposing to say about First London, I received a furious phone call from Derek Tread.

He had fallen out with Russell King; I inferred that from the reference to King which Tread himself used and which rhymed with runt.

"Fix this up Paul. This puts the whole North Korean deal in danger. I can't have these idiots running around allowing these kinds of comments to be made about us."

"Well, I'm not optimistic Derek. I've seen the guarantee and it really isn't a guarantee at all. What they say here in the copy is broadly correct…………"

I never had a chance to finish the legal explanation.

"*I don't fucking care.* Fix this up and get them to correct the story. That's what you're being paid for".

He was virtually screaming at me so I didn't think it was the right time to tell him I hadn't actually been paid anything at all yet. But the scream had stopped almost as suddenly as it started so getting off the phone before it started again was more of a priority:

"I'll see what I can do Derek".

He put the phone down without saying another word; so at least my immediate objective was achieved. As for the greater object, I drafted an e-mail to Matt Scott saying that First London was not prepared to comment on a legal opinion which the newspaper had clearly obtained from another firm of lawyers but the reality of the position was that Blenheim and the companies behind it were sufficiently strong financially so as to make any prospect of a default highly unlikely; it was equally unlikely, therefore, that the guarantee would ever be called on so it was something of a sterile exercise to debate its terms. I pointed out also that the guarantee was not triggered in the absence of a final court judgement for the relevant debt so that made a call even more unlikely.

That last bit was intended to shield First London as much as possible from the flak that the story would create; but in fact it was to draw it deeper into the article. When it was published the following day, it was obvious that the Digger was digging into the affairs of First London just as much as Notts County. Having recited virtually word for word the points which I had made the previous evening in my e-mail, the article went on:

"The First London balance sheet showed assets of £180 Million as at 31 March but the latest accounts filed by the company also reveal that at that point

285

First London held just £18,657 in cash and had only £1.3 million available to it in undrawn borrowings. It is unclear what First London's equity assets include but it enjoyed an impressive year to 31 March".

And then, as if that wasn't bad enough, it went on to enmesh First London into Notts County by reference to the ongoing SCH deal which, transparently, was Derek Tread's primary objective. He would not be happy and as soon as I saw the paper that morning I was already planning an unscheduled day off to avoid the storm. The article didn't pull any punches:

"Guardian investigations have revealed that there are individuals linked with both First London and Swiss Commodity Holding, the company in which the Notts County director of football, Sven- Goran Eriksson, believes he was promised shares as part of his inducement to join the club and whose logo is at the heart of the new Notts County club badge.

Representatives of Swiss Commodity Holding including Russell King were recently pictured meeting Kim Yong-Nam, effectively North Korea's Head of State in Pyongyang.

First London and First Commodity Holding also share a director, Nigel Little. Kevin Leech, a former Jersey bankrupt, is also a director of SCH. In First London's annual return in June this year it was revealed that 11% of First London is owned through a trust called Condor Ventures, whose owner is recorded as Kevin Leech in a separate filing that month.

On 16 October First London sold its asset management division to Swiss Commodity for £173 million.

Last year First London issued new shares to take over Bahrain Capital, a company which had connections with Russell King. Subsequent to that deal a company called Mirison Invest and Finance assumed a 44.35% share in First London. It is ultimately controlled by an entity called Amorogos Trust.

A spokesman for First London said: 'Russell King and Nathan Willett have no shareholding interest, whether directly or indirectly, in First London".

That was all strikingly accurate.

Now we were looking at a clusterfuck that tied up First London with Notts County with North Korea and Kevin Leech: Kevin Leech, the beginning of it all (for me) and, as the *Guardian* correctly put it, "former bankrupt", owner through his offshore trust of 11% of the shares in First London and a director of Swiss Commodity Holding. How was it even possible that the acquisition of First London by SCH could go ahead now? The file was still sitting on the desk of the Takeover Panel in London after the disclosure that Russell King had been involved in an insurance fraud; what was the Panel going to make of all of this? A former bankrupt owned 11% of the target and was in turn a director the company looking to buy the target;

and the target, First London, had cash assets of less than £19,000 and looked to have overstated its position in its accounts filed only eight months previously.

It wasn't looking good.

Despite my natural inclination to take the day off and hide from him I decided this was not an issue that was going away so I made my way up to the office with a heavy heart; and sure enough Derek Tread had already been calling. I took an emergency coffee and called him back. Amazingly, he was in a convivial mood:

"It's not as bad as it sounds".

Perhaps he had been drinking; had he seen the same article that I had?

"It does look pretty bad Derek".

"No, what we are going to do is to get King and Willett to sell out of the Project; in fact we've already done it. Kevin and I have been over to Bahrain and have had them sign over their interests. From here on they have nothing to do with First London or SCH. We are going to finish off this project without them. The Takeover Panel can go and fuck itself. Kevin is a director of SCH; he will take over the negotiations with the North Koreans and we'll get everything through on our own".

That all sounded fairly optimistic to me but it had a certain simplicity which was superficially attractive after all of the labyrinthine complexities of the deals we had been looking at over the past two months; and, best of all, he wasn't screaming at me. Anyway I really don't think that lawyers and professional advisers are always the best judges of things, sometimes their antennae can be sorely lacking. A good example of that is the meeting that I had with the main board of Mirror Group Newspapers on the evening of the day that we found out Robert Maxwell had stolen upwards of £600 Million from its pension funds (chicken feed by the standards of today's mega frauds). As the day had gone on and things had got bleaker and bleaker (*"another £200 million missing"*; virtually shouted around the door of the board room), I was joined by a partner from one of the major accounting firms and by an actuary whose job was to tell the board how much it would cost to fully fund the depleted pension schemes. The three of us were waiting for an hour or so in the corridor outside, waiting for the board to call on us in turn to advise on the catastrophe that was unwinding around us. It was literally chaotic, nobody knew whether this would be the last day of the *Daily Mirror's* distinguished life; whether it could survive this crisis, and as people ran up and down the corridor in front of us, carrying files and more bad news and dropping papers behind them, there was a fellow gradually and slowly rolling up the red carpet that ran from one end of the corridor to the other. We all three saw him coming slowly towards us, down on all fours rolling the carpet up; and we all three lifted our feet in turn as he got to us, so as to make it easier for him to keep on rolling; and then we all watched him as he slowly progressed to the other end of the corridor with the roll of carpet, get up and stretch his limbs and then walk off with it. He was in fact stealing it as a souvenir, no doubt thinking that he might as well get something out before the company collapsed into liquidation. We found out when one of the directors emerged to call us in:

"Where's the carpet?"

"Somebody took it away"

"Why?"

"We don't know".

We looked at each other sheepishly.

"Well, didn't you *ask* for God's sake? You mean you just sat there and watched him do it?"

We grew more sheepish, there was no answer to that.

"For fuck's sake! And *we're* supposed to be taking advice from *you*. Well, we don't have any choice, do we; we'll start with *you*......"

He pointed at the actuary, who stood up nervously. The director, seething with Scottish scorn, had already spun on his heels and gone back in without him.

The point being that however much you spend on expensive advice; legal, accounting or, if you are ever unlucky enough to need it, actuarial, you aren't exactly guaranteed common sense or astute business instincts from your team. Otherwise Mirror Group Newspapers would still have its red carpet.

The New Dawn

Kevin Leech (former bankrupt) is not a particularly sophisticated fellow; as I have said before, he was of Mancunian stock and such wiles as he had were imbued into him at an early age whilst he was working for and subsequently running his father's funeral business in Moss Side. He had an earthy charm and was very likeable but he wasn't likely to win any prizes for financial sophistication any time soon. So at first blush he was an odd choice to become they key operating director in Swiss Commodity Holding, incorporated in Geneva and apparently sitting on contracts worth in excess of £12 Billion. But that of course was exactly the point; the company was *sitting* on contracts, but they wouldn't actually be worth any hard cash until the resources they related to were brought out of the ground and sold; and as the resources themselves were all buried under the North Korean Countryside, that meant there would have to be negotiations with the North Korean Government to establish the basis on which they would be exploited. In short, the contracts were a start but no more than a preliminary to those exploitation talks. And it was Kevin Leech who they were proposing to send over to Pyongyang to sit down face to face with the North Korean officials to settle the necessary terms.

Lord knows what the North Koreans would make of Kevin Leech. At the best of times his cleft palate made it difficult for anyone with a normal grasp of spoken English to understand what he was saying.

But, be that as it may, Kevin was duly sent off to Pyongyang and we didn't hear anything from him for the next three weeks.

In the meantime there was work to do in London.

As presaged in the *Guardian* Article, First London had earlier that year sold off its asset management business to SCH, or, to be more precise, it had sold the business to interests of Russell King held through his Bahraini holding company. If King was, as Derek Tread had told me, now to be cut out of the deal altogether, then it would be necessary to transfer the asset management business back to First London and then to regain control of the First London shares which had been sold to King. In the day to day, rub along world of normal business, neither of those steps would be altogether straightforward.

Transactions of that scale (medium sized by SCH/ North Korean standards, but certainly substantial in themselves) would conventionally call for detailed negotiations and preparation of complex documentation; probably requiring teams of lawyers to work over several weeks. But you have to remind yourself that this was First London's world where nothing was quite what it seemed and Derek Tread had, almost literally, drawn up the entire deal (both parts of it) on the back of a fag packet. The terms which he had put together were not only very brief; they were also very curious. Russell King was to get nothing out of the transaction save an expectancy that in the fullness of time, when the assets in North Korea started to be exploited, he *might* be paid something. Why would he give up his shareholding interest in First London and get nothing in return beyond a vague hope that he might be paid something in the future? The answer was not immediately obvious; at least not to me it wasn't. Then what about the shareholders in First London; they had agreed to sell their asset management business in the first place on the basis that they would be paid £173 Million. When were they supposed to receive that money, because there was no suggestion at all that anything had been paid to them so far and I knew now for sure that there was no prospect whatsoever of them ever being paid anything by the Russell King faction. These were obviously major issues and no rational person would fail to try to nail them down with as much clarity as possible before allowing the deal to go final; but not Derek Tread, he just skated over them with a blithe indifference. He had no interest at all in even talking about them; because his mind was very obviously (and very firmly) still fixed on getting hold of all that North Korean gold; points such as these no more than "legalese" anyway. I had been down that particular road with him already.

Having read over his fag packet terms a couple of times I decided that I didn't want my firm's name to be anywhere near the resulting document. So I had his "notes" typed up on plain paper and sent the typed pages over to him. He could do what he wanted with them as far as I was concerned, provided nobody got the impression that either I or my Firm had put the terms together for him; cooked them up would be a better expression. Derek Tread had no objection to that and, as things transpired, he took the two stapled pages over to Bahrain that weekend and had King sign up to them; so reverting ownership of First London Asset Management at a stroke and forcing King out of First London for good. Russell King was clearly under some species of pressure to do that so readily (this was real money he was giving up after all); and I am pretty sure that it must have been more than the shame of the abortive BMW Sauber deal (he had no shame); or even the revelations of insurance frauds in *the Sun* (ditto). It seems to me that Derek Tread must have had something on him to make Russell King slink away so silently from the circus which he had, after all, put together with his own fat hands. But whatever it was, I never found out.

I almost felt sorry for Russell King; he was obviously being well and truly shafted by Derek Tread; I a*lmost* felt sorry, but not quite. This was after all the man mountain who had been responsible for cutting a swathe not only through my practice but also through others much more important than mine; including Rothschilds where the news had finally broken a week or so earlier that Meryick Cox had been sacked for making the imprudent statements which he had done in connection with the financial standing of Qadbak Investments. Russell King was leaving a trail of ruined careers behind him. He and Tread were two of a kind and they probably deserved each other. But the others who suffered from his delusions didn't; not Meyrick Cox or Peter Sauber or Peter Trembling or Sven Goran Eriksson; or, indeed, the thousands of Notts County fans who had been deluded into buying into Russell King's dream. None of them deserved to be subjected to his particular brand of insidious poison.

The last time I spoke with Russell King was when he called me up a couple of days before the fag packet terms had been sent over to me by Derek Tread. I had grown beyond weary with him by that stage so that our more recent conversations had become increasingly coloured by a crispy frostiness on my part:

"Paul, I need you to do something for me if that would be possible."

Silence.

"Shall I tell you what it is?"

He was obviously picking up some of the frost.

"OK Russell: tell me what it is."

"I would like you to incorporate thirty Cayman Island companies for me this afternoon, can you put that together? I can let you have a list of the names we are looking for to put on the companies".

He was still talking as though the circus was under his direction; blubbering out his directions to me; but of course it wasn't under his direction at all, not now; even as we spoke the circus was already in the process of moving on and Derek Tread was being measured up for the top hat and red tailcoat.

"If I do that I will need you to pay me in advance for the local fees in Cayman Russell; none of our bills have been paid and we are out of pocket on most of these transactions. Will you wire me the covering funds across by lunchtime?"

I was toying with him. I had asked him so often over the past weeks to send me over covering funds, that this (as it turns out the last) request was very much in the nature of twisting his tail. I wanted to see what he would say.

"Well, bear with me on this Paul, it might be difficult to organise a transfer to you that quickly. Could you put it together from your office account and I will make sure you are made good".

"No. I can't do that Russell."

"Why not? What's the problem?"

Blubber, blubber, blubbering……..God knows where he was talking from now, but he was seriously missing out on chutzpah; I doubted that the Dorchester would be extending any further credit to him.

"The *problem*, Russell, is that you have not been paying our fees and we are now seriously out of pocket. I don't think we can extend you any further credit by way of a transfer from our office account."

"But I need these companies set up urgently; Paul, be reasonable, this is for me here. I am not Qadbak or Munto; those are the companies that owe you fees on the other transactions, not me. Don't hold it against me. I'll do what I can to get them to pay you but I really need your help on this now. Can you do this for *me*?"

He sang out the word "*me*" in a kind of falsetto; a blubbery falsetto. As it happens I found out a couple of days later just why he wanted these companies to be set up in the Cayman Islands in such a hurry. Derek Tread told me.

"No, I'm afraid I can't do that Russell. Even if you could get me funding to cover the local fees, I really am not going to put my firm's name to setting up a series of nominee companies for you; not after all the stuff we've been through over the past two months. I'm sorry, but that's not going to happen."

Derek Tread told me later that the companies Russel King wanted to incorporate were to receive funding on his behalf from the SCH project; they would operate nominee bank accounts; this, in other words, was Russell King's kickback structure, entered into in return for getting out of SCH and handing over control to Derek Tread and Kevin Leech. I didn't know that at the time I spoke with King and turned his request down; if I had known then I would not have been so polite. I might have used earthier language, more Anglo Saxon.

"After all we've been through together Paul........."

Exactly; that was *exactly* the point. After all I had been through with this dystopian creature; after going through all of *that*, I wasn't now minded to regulate my dealings with Russell King with anything shorter than a very long barge pole.

"Yes, sorry Russell."

And that was that. He exited stage left, back in Bahrain within a matter of days and pursued by a number of international law enforcement authorities. I never spoke with Russell King again.

But, back to the narrative and the back of the fag packet deal; having got Russell King's signature on the deal Derek Tread and Kevin Leech now found themselves in control of Munto and, through it, Notts County Football Club. Talk about leaving the frying pan for the fire.

I am still not wholly sure how either of them exercised that control because neither of them were on the board of directors at the Club; and although it was true that Munto was a bearer share company in the British Virgin Islands so that it was owned by whoever happened to hold its shares from time to time (no doubt Tread or Leech or both), I couldn't quite see how that shareholding control could be converted into telling the Notts County Board what they should or shouldn't do. But however the two of them did it, and in the intervals between hard headed talks in Pyongyang, the future of the Club became a regular issue in our talks.

In particular that meant the future of Sven Goran Eriksson at the Club, where he was still director of football. Without him the Project was unlikely to get anywhere so it was a theme of my discussions with Tread and Leech that we should do whatever we could to make Eriksson content and stop him from walking away; and there was now a very real prospect that he *would* walk away.

When Eriksson had joined Notts County in June 2009 he had been given a five year contract to act as director of football, but he also had what was termed a "side agreement" under which he would act as an "ambassador" for SCH; under this side agreement he expected to receive a sum in excess of £2 Million which would be paid once the SCH takeover of First London was completed. He had been told by Russell King and Nathan Willett that the takeover of First London would be completed before the end of August 2009. It was now November and Sven wanted his £2 Million; he had served a formal notice requiring payment by the end of the month.

Sol Campbell had already left the Club, Russell King was in disgrace and the Club was facing a new investigation by the Football League into its opaque ownership structure. The fiasco of the BMW Sauber deal had discredited the Club still further and the press, notably in the shape of the Digger at the Guardian, were constantly snapping at the Board's heels. If Sven-Goran Eriksson were to leave now then that would undoubtedly sound the death knell for the Project. But how likely was it that SCH would be in a position to pay him £2 million? There was no chance of that happening and neither was First London in a position to fund the payment (it would be placed into insolvent liquidation within 8 months). But as ever, Tread and Leech were fixated on keeping the plates spinning as long as possible and their plan was for me to talk with Eriksson and tell him that everything was Russell King's fault and if he could only bear with them for a little while longer then through Kevin Leech's negotiations in Pyongyang, they would release the SCH funding and Sven would be paid in full.

So that was my brief.

I arranged a conference call with Eriksson and his business adviser and long term confidante Tord Grip. The substance of the call was instructive.

Despite his affable public persona, I actually found Eriksson to be very brittle and defensive when we spoke; perhaps that was not wholly surprising in the circumstances. He needed no telling from me that the villain of the piece was Russell King; the manner in which he spat out King's name left me in no doubt but that he regarded him as little short of the devil incarnate. Tord Grip would often have to intervene in the conversation to calm Eriksson down. I had the very clear impression that if Eriksson could have got his hands on King's blubbery frame then his life might have been in danger. But Grip was doing a reasonable job of keeping Eriksson under control; right down to the point where we talked about money:

"I'm afraid we are pretty sure Sven that Qadbak Investments is not a substantial entity; it won't be in a position to make any payments to you and I don't think you ought to hold any store by getting anything from that quarter in the near future".

There was a short silence.

"I don't understand anything you are saying".

I had thought, if only from Match of the Day, that Eriksson had a reasonably good grasp of English. Tord grip was telling me to slow my delivery down, but I decided to simplify it as well:

"Mr Eriksson, you will not be getting any money from Qadbak Investments. That company is not worth anything...It has nothing".

He understood that alright:

"But that cannot be the case. Coutts who are my bankers carried out a full investigation into Qadbak and they reported that I could rely on them."

Tord Grip, like me, thought that was unlikely and pointed out that the Coutts report had only concluded that there was no reason to distrust Qadbak; not that it could be actually trusted. I knew what Grip meant by that but I am sure to Sven-Goran Eriksson and indeed the rest of the English speaking world, such distinctions were mere sophistry. In any event his tone didn't change:

"I don't understand. That can't be the case. I trusted this company...."

He seemed to run out of steam and now had the tone of a child who has been promised jelly for pudding but gets a left over rusk.

"I understand that Mr Eriksson but I think we are all keen to move forward as best we can; obviously Russell King has a lot to answer for......"

"Russell King......."

He spat but didn't finish his sentence.

"Let me tell you where we are at the moment. There was an intention to structure a takeover of First London by SCH and, had that happened, it would have released the funds that would have been required to meet the payment that was due to you under the side agreement; to do that within the two months that you were expecting. But for a lot of reasons, some of them to do with the way in which Russell King has behaved..........."

I waited to give him an opportunity to spit the name out again, but Sven had fallen silent.

"....some of which, as I say, had to do with the way in which Russell King behaved; it won't now be possible to secure the acquisition in the way we had intended; so the intention is that SCH will itself negotiate with the authorities in North Korea to put together the terms under which the relevant mineral rights will be exploited; Kevin Leech is in North Korea at the moment beginning that process. Have you met Kevin Leech......?"

No answer.

"Kevin Leech is in Pyongyang at the moment to start that process off and we are hopeful that he will have made sufficient progress for us to let you have a reliable timeline for the release of the funding either before Christmas or early in January……….."

He was still saying nothing.

"So, speaking from the perspective of the Football Club and of the SCH Project generally, Mr Eriksson, I hope we can rely on you to bear with us just a while longer so that we can release the funds that are needed to meet the commitments that were made to you."

"I'll think about it…….."

I felt he forced those words out of himself. They were the last words I heard from him because after a few cursory goodwill comments he hung up without saying anything else and I never heard from him after that. I wasn't inspired with any deep seated conviction that he was likely to stay on at the Club and indeed he didn't.

As Yeats might well have put it, things then fell apart, the centre couldn't hold any longer. For a start, the tax man hadn't gone away; not by any means. The few short weeks which the Club had managed to buy with Peter Trembling's £100,000 had expired weeks ago leaving us all; lawyers, Club and accountants subject to the daily toothache grind of letters and phone calls from the man at the Inland Revenue; and however much of a specialist he was in football matters, it was money and not football that was closest to his heart. At the best of times this fellow was miserable and gloomy to the point of asphyxiation, with his constant predictions of bankruptcy and financial collapse unless the Revenue was paid its Danegeld, you could almost hear the dust falling off his mourning coat, but now he was positively deadly:

"But Mr Fallon, you know the Club has to pay this money; and your client must know that as well, so why aren't they paying it?"

The answer should have been obvious even to him; the Club wasn't paying it because it didn't have the money to pay; but, of course, I couldn't say that to him, not in any way which would be consistent with my obligations to the client. So instead I regularly resorting simply to begging for mercy; begging in every way that I could think of short of actually going down on my knees (and I would have done that too but for my bad legs):

"Please understand me, both the Club and we are doing everything we can to deal with this situation; it's not as though we aren't treating the commitment as important, you've already had £100,000 as a show of our good faith; and that was the figure that *you* asked for not me. As you said at the time, paying £100,000 would allow us time to look over the numbers and find out the right figure; and once the Club has established what the right figure is, we will of course pay that to you."

That was pretty good begging; but he wasn't buying it.

"Well, what has your client been doing to establish the correct figure since the end of October; could you at least tell me that?"

That was a barbed question; and he knew it. I couldn't tell him that we had appointed investigating accountants in mid-October but that they had been sacked by Russell King for being "useless"; and even then, not before expressing a "*firm preliminary view*" that the figure which the Inland Revenue were asking for was properly due and payable. Maybe it was precisely because the accountants had arrived at this view at all that Russell King had decided to sack them. That, of course, was a very distinct possibility. In the nature of the dialogue I was engaged in with the Revenue though, it was necessary to draw a veil over all of that:

"All I can tell you is that the Club has been working flat out to deal with this issue, it is important, we know that; but I hope you understand that we are dealing with all this just as quickly as we can. As I say, we have already, at *your* suggestion, sent you a substantial payment as a sign of our good faith."

I was playing my best card again. It wasn't a particularly good card, but it was the best I had; and once again, it didn't work:

"I don't want good faith Mr Fallon; I want the tax that is due to be paid. You aren't giving me any options here......."

I knew what was coming next. It would be the latest of many such threats:

"...........we are going to have to issue a winding up petition as a preliminary to putting the Club into liquidation."

Surprise sur-*fucking* prise.

Our man at the Revenue was as predictable and as one directional as a snake in a waggon rut.

Say what you want about them though, the Revenue have written their own play book over the years and they stick to it pretty much to the letter. I remember that I was phoned up by them one day when I was running my own law firm. The young lady told me that they were planning to conduct a raid on our office to ensure VAT compliance; fair enough, there was no reason why we shouldn't pay our VAT, as indeed we did. But why were they planning a *raid*? She didn't say, just that they were planning one and that it was scheduled for execution in the second week of October; this was the middle of *June*. I didn't ask her why we were getting four months' notice. There was no need to look a gift horse in the mouth. Then she asked me whether we were on the ground floor of our building; we weren't; so did we have a lift because it was possible that one or more members of their raiding team might be suffering from a disability so that they wouldn't be able to make the stairs. Yes, we had a lift I told her. I could hear her making a note for the raid planning schedule. Then she wanted to know whether we kept any animals in the office; because, for similar reasons, one or more of the members of the raiding team might be allergic to animal hair. I was tempted to tell her that we kept a horse in the office but I resisted the temptation; I suspected that irony and humour were not the best tools to use with these folk. They were more than ironic and humorous enough as it was without any help from me.

The Revenue might work out of an office in Liverpool called The Triad (seemingly without any sense of irony), but they lack the spontaneous unpredictability of organised crime and move instead on well-worn rails. There is simply no point in trying to divert them from their purpose. All they ever want is money.

And that is exactly what Notts County didn't have, so the Revenue duly issued their winding up petition later that week; and, as I had advised Russell King and Peter Trembling the previous month, this had the immediate effect of freezing the Club's bank accounts and making its creditors run for cover. There would be no more credit and the small army creditors who had assembled already wouldn't be waiting for payment of what they were already due; and that included the players who, in common with most of the Club's employees, were almost all due outstanding salary so that Notts County had effectively been running on their goodwill for the past month. Now the goodwill was exhausted. The creaking structure that Russell King and Nathan Willett had put in place at Meadow Lane was fatally holed beneath the waterline.

Russell King was already back in Bahrain and Nathan Willet followed him.

In a desperate last ditch attempt to salvage something from the wreckage Peter Trembling bought the Club for £1; but he wasn't able to provide the funding that it so desperately needed and eventually the Revenue saw him off too, there was still a mountain of unpaid tax to pay and nothing short of a full throated serious rescue attempt would do. It came, as it happens, from a local businessman called Ray Trew who bought the Club in February 2010. I met him once and he seemed a very fair minded and well-grounded fellow; the exact opposite of Russell King and exactly what the Club needed. The Club never made it into the Premiership after all and I lost my bet (even if I could find the betting slip now which I can't); but I am glad the Club is now doing well, or at least as well as can be expected. At least it is rid of the poison.

And then…….

It was, as I have said, an extraordinary period in my
life. I still don't know what Russell King thought he
was doing; perhaps he derived some kind of bizarre
satisfaction from feeling that he was, even for a brief
period, ringmaster of a peculiar circus where each of
the characters were orchestrated by him at one time or
another (as indeed we all were); or perhaps it was no
more than the fantasy of a fat man sunk too deep in a
world of habitual lies ever to rise to the regular
surface without professional help. Either way, when
the lies at SCH, at Notts County and Sauber got too
much for him, as at the end of the day they were
bound to, he took flight back to his bolt hole in
Bahrain. As best I know he is still there today.

Various jurisdictions have issued warrants for his
arrest including Jersey. It has been suggested in some
press reports that he is held under house arrest in
Bahrain, but maybe his bulk means he is simply no
longer able to get out of the front door. Who knows?
BBC Television ran a special investigation on Russell

King in its *Panorama* Programme and caught fleeting footage of him trying to shut his front door on their reporter; the programme also suggested that the Serious Fraud office in London wanted Russell King's help with their inquiries. I suspect that much at least is true. The sheer scale of the wreckage he left behind was simply too much for that not to happen. But, again as best I know, nobody in England has brought him back for questioning yet. Time will tell.

First London collapsed into liquidation in 2010, so the witches den in St James's Square is no more. That is probably for the good. It was always a throwback to the world of edgy financial institutions living on the brink of triumph or disaster. I am glad it is not there anymore to suck anyone else in. The liquidator of First London issued a press report saying that he had recommended misfeasance claims be brought in connection with the disposal agreements entered into in 2009; specifically the agreement relating to First London Asset Management. I am not surprised. There were a lot of things, I am sure, that need looking into there. Maybe they will be.

Then there is Kevin Leech, my old pal. He eventually disappeared into North Korea where for years he was apparently still trying to raise funds on the back of the SCH Asset Agreement; the *Guardian* (his old bête noir) ran an article in 2013 which commented critically on him and the pie in the sky quality of this, his last great project which he was still clinging to. Kevin had shuttled for long periods between China and North Korea and was, so he told me, the proud holder of a North Korean passport. But we don't speak any more. He had a kind heart, almost alone out of everyone involved in these sorry episodes and I am sorry that things went badly for him in the end; he was so very determined to demonstrate to the world that he still had it in him to succeed despite the blight of his bankruptcy. But I for one was never in any doubt about that; I always thought Kevin had it in him and I wish him well. I am though sure now, as I am confident he will be (in his heart at least), that all those old dreams were always too good to be true. That was my first instinct on that summer's day back in 2009 when he told me about North Korean Gold for the first time in the pub by the River Thames; so in a way we were both right in the end.

Printed in Great Britain
by Amazon.co.uk, Ltd.,
Marston Gate.